365 SOCIAL MEDIA POST IDEAS FOR REALTORS:

A REAL ESTATE MARKETING

PLAYBOOK

365 SOCIAL MEDIA CONTENT IDEAS & MARKETING TIPS
FOR REALTORS, REAL ESTATE AGENTS & BROKERS
TO GENERATE MORE LEADS ONLINE

NICK TSAI

BONUSES

Bonus 1- 10X Leadgen Virtual Bootcamp

Join our online Bootcamp to learn how you can generate more leads online with digital marketing, sign up now at: https://soldouthouses.com/10xleadgenbootcamp

Bonus 2- The Ultimate Real Estate Marketing Checklist

This checklist features 86 marketing tips to generate more leads online & offline.

Download your free checklist at
https://soldouthouses.com/checklist

TABLE OF CONTENTS

INTRODUCTION

Thanks for getting this book.

You made a wise decision because the book will enable you to create engaging social media content quickly and easily.

The 365 social media post ideas are designed to copy and paste into your social media profile.

So you can save both time and money when it comes to content.

And after reading this book, you will want to **take action fast.**

Let me ask you a question.

Would you like me to help you increase your results 10x by passing along my done-for-you Canva templates?

When it comes to social media marketing, photo posts consistently outperform text-only posts.

That's why I always recommend my clients use Canva-a free online design software-to create their social media posts.

For this, you have a few options.

First, you can do everything yourself and spend 10 to 20 minutes to create a single post. And that's if you know what you're doing. So it adds up to about 120 hours to create all 365 days of social media posts yourself.

Second, you can hire a designer to do it for you. It won't be cheap, considering a professional designer typically charges $25 to $50 per hour. That could cost up to $6000.

Or you can take advantage of my 365 done-for-you real estate social media posts.

This package turned the same 365 ideas you will see in the book into done-for-you Canva templates that you can easily plug in and play.

And the best part is you don't have to pay $6000 for the design, nor $600, and not even $100.

You will be able to turn everything you see in the book into engaging social media posts in the next 3 minutes without costing an arm and a leg.

You can go to the website https://soldouthouses.com/365doneforyoucontent to claim your special offer.

Who Am I?

Hi, my name is Nick Tsai. I'm a digital marketing expert, and I have over ten years of marketing experience.

Ten years ago, I was a realtor. As a rookie, I struggled to get clients even though I followed the traditional advice from the industry:

- Distributing flyers
- Posting classified ads

- Cold calling
- Cold mailing

But nothing worked for me.

I was frustrated, tired of struggling, and hopeless. I worked 12-hour days every day and still got no clients. I eventually burned out and quit. I lost my confidence, and self-doubt crept in.

Those were the worst days of my life.

Then one day, I received a phone call that changed everything.

It was from a stranger who wanted me to help him sell this house.

I had never called him, never mailed him, and didn't even know who he was.

But, for some reason, he found my website.

It was an ugly blog I used as a personal notebook where I wrote down everything I learned about real estate.

It became the #1 ranking real estate blog in my local area for some strange reason.

In the next few months, people kept calling. They asked me about real estate and even begged to be taken on as clients.

Suddenly, I became the go-to expert in the local area.

And getting clients became effortless.

It was an "aha" moment for me and

I realized, "It's easier to attract clients than to chase clients."

In the past, I pursued potential clients by cold calling, cold mailing, and sending flyers (aka junk mail). As a result, I became an annoying salesperson.

But by harnessing the power of the internet, I can easily reach people who are ready to buy and can position myself as an expert!

So, I decided to dive into internet marketing to discover how I could attract more clients online. I studied countless marketing books, attended marketing seminars, and learned from the best marketing experts in the world.

And that's why I set up Soldouthouses.com so realtors like I once can get results with digital marketing.

You can go to Soldouthouses.com to learn more about my products and services.

PART 1 - 365 DONE-FOR-YOU SOCIAL MEDIA CONTENT IDEAS

The first part of this book is 365 social media post ideas.

All the content in this part is written for the social media context, which means you can easily plug in and play for your social media marketing.

You can either copy and paste these ideas, customize them for your local area or create a post image.

And if you want to use them on an image-based social media platform, such as Instagram, you definitely will need to create post images for them; I highly recommend Canva - powerful free software that helps you to quickly get the job done.

Also, if you are too busy to create this content yourself, my team has turned all 365 social media ideas into done-for-you Canva templates; you can go to https://soldouthouses.com/365doneforyoucontent to check them out and get all of them for a special discount.

100 Real Estate Buying Tips

1. Fatten up your savings.

The last thing you want is to find a house you love only to learn that your savings aren't high enough yet. Buying your dream house but feeling less financially secure afterward is never a pleasant experience. So before you even start your home search, make sure you save enough first.

2. Buy in a place familiar to you.

It is not enough to just fall in love with the house itself. The neighborhood where it is located must also be equally lovable. Feeling unsure and not being familiar with the area are some of the top red flags that every home buyer should watch out for.

3. Don't take the idea of renting out of the equation.

Sometimes buying a house is not the best option for everyone. You might be better off renting a house, especially if you only plan to stay there for a few years. Your personal financial standing must also be considered to know if you can really afford to buy in the first place.

4. Know the best time to sell your current house.

Selling your current house is the first step when buying a new home. Make sure you know when it is more likely for people to list their homes and use it as your guide to determine when you should purchase your next home.

5. Put a limit on your budget.

Avoid buying a property worth $500,000 just because you were approved for a mortgage for that amount. Always remember that there are still other expenses involved in buying a house, such as taxes, closing costs, monthly bills, insurance, and repairs.

6. Research about things real estate agents won't probably tell you.

Whether you like it or not, real estate agents don't always divulge everything they know that you should know, too. Spend some time researching the local market to help you reach a wise buying decision when you are finally ready to make a purchase.

7. There is no guarantee of appreciation.

Housing markets can ebb and flow, which means that you won't always make money just because you are ready to sell. There is no guarantee of appreciation as far as residential real estate is concerned so always think long-term before you buy.

8. Set a time for a home inspection.

It might be quite tempting to forego a home inspection just because the house looks faultless. However, it is always worth investing in home inspections that can flag issues that you might not see otherwise and give you peace of mind as the buyer.

9. Don't forget to seek pre-approval.

You should seek pre-approval from lenders if you want sellers to take you seriously during your search for a house to buy. It will let sellers know right away that you have already taken the necessary financial steps to be qualified for a mortgage.

10. Learn more about down payments.

Depending on the lender, you will be required to give a down payment that is at least 5% of the selling price of the property. You also need to have some cash on hand as an emergency fund and for closing costs.

11. Shop around.

It is great if you fall in love with the first house you find, but it wouldn't hurt to check out as many homes as you can. It is a must to view several more houses to let you compare the strengths and weaknesses of each.

12. Gauge the limitations of your DIY skills.

Always consider exactly what you can and cannot handle if you will buy a house that requires repairs and maintenance. If some work is required on the property, make sure you also know the costs associated with the necessary repairs.

13. Get a second or even a third opinion.

When looking at a house to buy, sometimes it will work in your favor if you get a second or even a third opinion first. A family member or a friend might be able to pinpoint things you didn't notice or see.

14. Determine what you can and cannot live with.

Consider the things you can and cannot live with, especially if this is your first house. List all of your must-haves and those that you want but may not be absolutely necessary at the moment.

15. Don't let your emotions overpower you.

While it can be very exciting to buy a house, the process can also become stressful, especially in competitive markets. Make sure your emotions are always in check to ensure that you don't deal with expensive problems or overpay for a house.

16. Shop by season.

Ask real estate agents and they will surely tell you that homes are priced higher during summer or early spring. However, take note that there are still more factors to consider even if you buy in the right season. You may have less competition during winter but there might also be fewer properties to choose from.

17. Avoid judging based on things you see alone.

Some houses may look horrible with old carpets, peeling paint, and musty odors. However, just because the property looks bad doesn't always mean that there is no value in its current condition. When viewing a property, check under the carpets, inspect the foundation, and more.

18. Schedule multiple viewings.

Once you find a house that you like and you have more time to consider giving your offer, such as during the low season, make sure you visit the property several times before making your final decision. For example, view the house on a sunny day and a rainy day separately to know if you can live in the house all year round.

19. Work with an agent.

Employ a real estate agent if you are really serious about buying a house. This professional will not just schedule the showings and accompany you there because they can also guide you during the whole buying process. Also, since the seller pays their commission, it means you can use their service for free.

20. Know the difference between pre-approval and pre-qualification.

Make sure a credit union or bank pre-approves you before you start going to house viewings. You also need to get pre-approval rather than pre-qualification alone, which is just a preliminary letter from the bank with no official credit check and others.

21. Check that old paint.

Be wary of lead-based paint, especially if the house you plan to buy was constructed before 1978. You can use a lead paint test kit during one of your viewings to confirm this.

22. Go through the final walkthrough.

Many purchase agreements consent to a final walkthrough of a property to make sure that it is still in good shape. It may not seem necessary at first, but if you plan to buy a foreclosed property or you will displace unhappy renters, you have to make sure that there are no damages done at the last minute.

23. Talk to the neighbors.

Neighbors in some communities may affect your decision to buy a home. A good neighborhood can make it easy for you to meet a new friend, babysitter, or even a confidant. Neighbors can even provide background about past tenants or owners and possible damages they made.

24. Never force anything.

If you are excited about purchasing a house, it is all too easy to imagine yourself living in the one you like, despite it not being the right house for you. Avoid forcing anything just because you like the house itself or the community.

25. Consider the appraisal fee.

The appraisal fee usually runs from $300 up to $500 and shows up on a good faith estimate or loan estimate. This is often paid out of pocket, although there are times when it can be included in closing.

26. Check the need for a survey fee.

The survey fee covers property line verification and ensuring the right location of the fences. This fee is not a requirement in all states.

27. Conduct a flood determination assessment.

Flood determination assessments are often about $10 to $20 and help lenders identify if a certain property is located in a flood zone. This is necessary for lenders to confirm if the house has the right amount of insurance.

28. Know what an escrow fee is.

The closing fee is paid to the attorney, title company, or escrow company that conducts the closing. The presence of a real estate attorney at every closing is sometimes required in certain states. The escrow deposit is separate from the escrow fee.

29. Watch out for application fees.

Certain lenders use the mortgage application fee worth $400 up to $500 to make a home buyer commit to them. However, this is considered an excess fee that you should avoid at all costs.

30. Look into the credit report fee.

It is required for mortgage lenders to conduct a credit report on you if you have plans to buy a house. Sometimes, they will try charging you for this report for a price worth $30 to $50.

31. Research the origination fee.

The origination fee is often collected as a part of the closing costs following the approval of a loan. This is about .5% to 1% of the sale price. This fee often covers the cost of calculations, verifications, and paperwork to determine the mortgage.

32. Be familiar with the attorney fee.

Every attorney has a different rate, but it often costs approximately $400 to hire an attorney and involve them in the loan transaction.

33. Have some knowledge about the mortgage broker fee.

Remember that it will cost you the moment you decide to hire a mortgage broker. Mortgage brokers assist their clients in finding a loan, but they also charge 1% to 2% of the purchase price of the property.

34. Prepare to pay the prepaid interest.

Starting from the time you close to the time you make your first payment for your mortgage, lenders will probably expect you to pay an interest that accumulates during this period. You sometimes need to pay for it upfront during closing.

35. Know the state recording fee.

You need to record the sale of the property with the local government. This means that it is only normal to expect that this will also be associated with some fees. Always check with the government of your city and country to know more about these fees.

36. Be aware of the lender's title insurance.

The lender's title insurance, also called a loan policy, is required by lenders to keep themselves protected if there is an ownership claim on the property after its sale or an error shows up during the title search.

37. Be informed about the owner's title insurance.

A home seller can buy the owner's title insurance to offer them protection if there are title issues or there are ownership claims made on the specific property in question.

38. Determine when to heed advice from other people.

People will always have their opinions the moment you start searching for a property to buy. However, make sure you only listen to those who offer grounded advice and ignore everyone else. Listen to those who work in the industries of real estate, title, and home improvement because they know their stuff.

39. Never buy bigger than what you need.

It might feel too tempting but avoid buying a bigger space compared to what you really need at the moment. A bigger house means paying higher utility bills, maintaining more space, and being responsible for more stuff that can go wrong.

40. Use your pre-approval number as your guide.

It is never a guarantee once you get pre-approved for a loan. However, this can give you a better idea of the kind of mortgage that best suits you, which makes it an important step. The mortgage approval numbers also dictate the down payment amount you need, often around 20% but this varies for certain government FHA loans and the individual deals made with the sellers.

41. Pay attention to what your home inspector tells you.

Home inspections are not only a formality because they uncover serious problems such as pest issues, rot, foundation issues, improper insulation, roof damage, outdated wiring, improper insulation, and more. Knowing these issues is a must before making a final decision.

42. Get a feel for the area.

Don't miss out on the chance to go for a stroll, walk around a few blocks, and see the things there are to see. Assess the neighborhood and if you feel uneasy with the things you see, you might need to have second thoughts about buying a property there.

43. Take into account the age of the appliances.

Appliances are among the most expensive features of a house, which makes them more than deserving of a closer inspection. Replacement time is just around the corner if the appliance is already more than 10 years old in general.

44. Consider proximity to schools and work.

Make sure you check all the routes to nearby schools and work as needed. You also need to take note if there are public transportation stops in the area. Just looking at the map alone is not enough here. Travel all the routes personally to see how busy they are, what they are like, and how long the commute time takes.

45. Take note of the direction of the windows.

This detail may seem small, but it is surprisingly important as this dictates the amount of sun that the house will get, the time it will get it, and how hot the space can become once you keep the windows open.

46. Study the association details.

Check for the presence of an HOA or something similar to it. If there is one, go through all their requirements and take note of the fees and their specific coverage. See if it is allowed to change anything about the house or park a trailer or vehicle.

47.Look into other offers.

Find out if the house has other current or expected offers. It is also good to know to look into who is bidding on the house if possible. For instance, an investor often offers cash up front, making counter offers more difficult.

48.Take advantage of an inspection to reduce risk.

The purchase of your first home is probably the most expensive purchase you will ever make and this involves a mind-boggling amount of details. You can reduce some of the risks for a 30-year mortgage you will assume when you buy the house if you hire an independent home inspector.

49.Be confident in your first home purchase.

Working with a home inspector will give you another opportunity to go through their decision before they buy their first house. Signing a purchase agreement in a competitive home-selling market with no home inspection will mean a done deal with no recourse for the buyer.

50.Learn about the ROI of home inspection.

It costs around $400 to hire a home inspector. However, the return on investment, or ROI, in hiring these professionals is significant considering the amount you can save as a buyer in the long term.

51. Work with the right home inspector.

Ask your family and friends to find a reliable home inspector. Determine if someone in your personal network has had inspections done in the past. After you talk to your own circle, do a quick search online to look into the online presence and reviews of the home inspectors.

52. Ask your realtor about a home inspection.

If this is your first time buying a home, make sure you inquire about the home inspection process with your realtor. Don't forget to also ask for their opinion as to what the home inspector should focus on depending on your specific needs.

53. Conduct a pre-inspection of your own.

A mere look at the house can make you learn so many things about it. Don't miss the chance to do your own pre-inspection and take note of any potential problems. Go through the interior and exterior of the house to spot any issues that need your attention.

54. List the specific things you would want to be checked during the inspection.

Itemize every single part that you want your home inspector to check first. If there is anything that you think requires a closer inspection, don't hesitate to inform the inspector about it.

55. Prepare for the inspection.

Once you have finally chosen a home inspector, it is only natural to have a long list of questions in mind. Jot down your questions in a notebook and prepare your camera and tape measure that you will bring with you during the actual inspection.

56. Be present during the inspection.

While other homebuyers skip attending the entire inspection, doing so might be your perfect opportunity to learn new things about the property and view it in a different light. This will let you experience the house for some time with no interruptions whatsoever.

57. Check the exterior while considering the weather conditions.

An important part of any home inspection is checking the exterior of the property. Since you will spend at least half an hour outside, be sure to consider the weather and wear the right clothing. Windows, siding, landscape grading, and foundation are some major areas of concern you need to check.

58. Take photos as proof.

The best home inspectors use a camera during the inspection. Ask the inspector to take photos of any possible problems that may arise so you will be able to see these with your own eyes and ensure that you have a better understanding of the problem and how to solve them accordingly.

59. Look beyond the small details.

While a few cosmetic blemishes might require your attention, remember that the main purpose of a home inspection is to find less obvious but potentially expensive repairs, such as water damage in the basement or structural issues.

60. Let an expert go over any missed areas during the inspection.

It also wouldn't hurt to get another pair of eyes to go over the house, especially since home inspectors don't always catch everything. Experts can check wells, septic tanks, and underground pipes that are all expensive to replace or repair.

61. Inspect the wiring.

Aluminum wiring is common in houses constructed during the mid-1960s or 1970s. If this is the case with the house you are planning to buy, confirm if everything is retrofitted properly. This will prevent fire hazards while letting you save thousands of dollars on replacement wiring.

62. Have the GFCIs tested out.

GFCI outlets are an important building code aspect in rooms with existing moisture. The inspector knows how to test the outlets correctly and any broken or malfunctioning GFCI outlets may indicate more serious electrical issues.

63. Do your homework.

Doing more research is a very important step that you can never take for granted. Knowing all of your different loan options and being familiar with the costs associated with a home purchase are things that need careful and in-depth research on your part.

64. Buy the right size for your needs.

Many home buyers end up regretting not purchasing a bigger house. Try to pick a house with a size that suits your current needs and your anticipated needs in the future.

65. Consider future developments.

Think about possible developments in the future once you find that perfect house you want. Check for potential road expansions and more houses to be built and who will move in them. While getting your hands on such concrete information may not be easy, you can find the right house if you consider some what-ifs.

66. Ponder on the commute time.

The commute to and from work may become a burden at one point. Choose a house closer to your workplace if your commute uses most of the time that you should have spent with your family or on your personal goals.

67. Choose a realtor you are comfortable working with.

Having a connection with your realtor is a must. A realtor must be authentic, honest, and patient, with the willingness to educate and guide you in every step of the homebuying process. If possible, try to talk to past clients of the realtor to get an idea of their experience.

68. Make location your top priority.

More than anything else, the location of the house you want to buy will help maintain its value regardless of the market conditions. Check the amenities in the neighborhood, public transit access, recreation areas, and the presence of busy streets.

69. Choose a house with a garage.

If you want to maintain the value of your chosen home, make sure it has a one-car garage instead of not having any garage at all. It will be better if you have two garage stalls although one will still do.

70. Study ranch or rambler houses.

Ramblers are among the home styles that any first-time homebuyer should consider. These are plain houses constructed in the mid-1900s with the potential of giving you more square footage for every dollar. You can find these houses in inner-ring suburbs and they can be transformed into amazing one-level dwellings.

71. Don't dismiss split-level houses.

Ruling out split-entry houses may make you miss out on an affordable home with excellent features. Split-level houses also often have three bedrooms on their upper floors, which are amenities that can help maintain the value of the home.

72. Don't trust the price estimates you find on Zillow.

Zillow only serves as a starting point in determining the value of a property. Their estimated values are derived from a proprietary formula that uses user-submitted and public data. Don't mistake those numbers for bank appraisal.

73. Establish a connection with the seller.

Getting personal with the seller can go a long way, especially if you want to be sure that you will stand out once the bidding war starts. Talk to them in person or send them a letter that talks more about your family and what makes the house and neighborhood suitable for your needs.

74. Don't neglect the roof.

The roof of any home plays an important role in keeping its interior in tip-top shape. This also happens to be the part of the house that is most labor-intensive and expensive to replace. Check the last time the roof was replaced and if it is backed by a warranty or not.

75. Watch out for cosmetic repairs.

New floors and a fresh coat of paint are usually signs that the seller cares about the house they are selling. However, there are times when these fixes are merely cosmetic cover-ups to hide underlying issues. Pay attention to suspicious fixes, and ask the inspector to look at them closely.

76. Look around the attic.

An attic that functions properly is important for a home's protection. You can usually learn so much about the house and the need for any repairs or renovations if the home inspector can reach the attic without squashing insulation.

77. Try the plumbing system

A slow drain or loss of water pressure are often signs of more serious plumbing concerns. Test the shower pans and bathtubs for any leaks. Ask the home inspector to examine the water shut-off and main points.

78. Learn the details about the water heater and furnace.

Aside from making sure that the water heater and furnace are working properly, you also need to know the age of each one as well as when it was last serviced. It can be expensive to replace these features so having them checked is a wise decision.

79. Scrutinize the basement.

Unfinished basements can give you plenty of clues regarding the condition of the foundation and the house in general. Look out for water issues, signs of repairs, and cracks. While cracks are not always deal breakers, knowing why there is a crack in the first place is a must.

80. Deal with projects one by one.

While it can be quite tempting to try to do everything at once, turning the entire house upside down will only add more to your stress levels later on. You will be better off tackling one project at a time, not to mention that it will also help you save more in the long run.

81. Verify things.

Be sure to ask the seller for full written disclosures regarding mold, leaks, old damage, repairs, remodeling, and more. Check with a county or city and get in writing the permit history, prior uses, zoning, HOA restrictions, and everything else about the property. Verify everything to save yourself from costly mistakes.

82. Know the crime stats.

Don't sign on that dotted line just yet until you get a complete report of the police calls that the neighborhood gets. For all you know, the house is probably being sold off at a bargain price because of the area's high crime rates, which is a big no-no.

83. Make sure a home warranty is in place.

Asking the seller to include a home warranty in the deal can help you save a lot of money if ever you need any repairs or fixes around the house.

84. Seek recommendations from neighbors about their trusted professionals.

Your neighbors are your best resource if you are looking for electricians, plumbers, and other pros. Those who are living near you are the right people who can give you the sound advice you need.

85. Make an offer for the tools.

You might be in for a great deal if you are buying from a family that is planning to downsize. You can save more if you offer to also buy their existing tools in the house such as the garden tools, snowblowers, tractors, etc.

86. Set aside money for unexpected issues.

If you buy a house with an old furnace, you can pretty much expect that it will break down some time soon. Saving enough money will make sure that you are ready for such significant dents on your finances.

87. Work with a buyer's agent.

Buying a house can be a very challenging process if you don't seek the help of a buyer's agent. Your agent will serve as your exclusive representative. To make things even better, the seller is the one who pays the agent, making it a win-win situation for you.

88. Be careful with hiring a dual agent.

Working with a dual agent might not always work in your favor. Some states even consider dual agents illegal or restricted. Dual agents represent the seller and the buyer alike during the transaction.

89. Know more about any easements.

Anyone granted an easement is also granted the legal right of using the property. However, the landowner still retains the land's legal title. Understand any easements on the property to know what to expect once you start living there.

90. Prepare earnest money.

Earnest money, also called a good faith deposit, is the best way of showing the seller how serious you are about purchasing the house. The money shows the buyer's willingness to sacrifice cash to put into the down payment of a home, hopefully securing the purchase of the property.

91. Look into seller concessions.

A seller concession is a deal, monetary gift, or other agreement that benefits the seller and buyer alike. This is applicable to the repair or closing costs. A concession is probably the result of an inspector report's findings, such as electrical wiring issues or a damaged roof.

92. Hire an attorney for title curation.

See to it that you work with an attorney whose specialty is title curation. It is recommended to have a title curation expert proactively involved right away after the discovery of a defect or issue in the title of the property.

93. Be familiar with TRID.

TRID is the lending regulation that helps borrowers have a full understanding of their loans' terms. This is an effort to assist borrowers to learn the actual value of borrowing with stringent disclosure timelines on the utility readings and the disclosure of financing terms to the buyers or borrowers.

94. Understand limits on renovations.

Many people seem to assume that they can already do anything they want with a house when they become its owner. However, you still need to consider HOA requirements and municipal regulations before proceeding with any renovation projects.

95. Study all the insurance options.

Most mortgages require homeowners to carry specific insurance amounts, which are necessary since replacing a house can be very expensive. Getting insurance sooner than later will work to your advantage in the long run.

96. Timing the market is impossible.

Instead of trying to time the real estate market, you should focus instead on finding the home that best suits you and your family's needs. This will make sure that you will be happier living in the house for many years to come.

97. The best mortgage doesn't always have the lowest interest rate.

Don't let the lowest interest rate fool you into thinking that it is already the best mortgage. Be sure to work with a mortgage lender with a good understanding of the business and help you reach your ultimate goal of closing on a property.

98. Stick to your buying budget.

Never let your emotions get the best of you. Avoid going over your set budget for your home purchase no matter how perfect it may seem to you. See to it that your budget also includes enough money for renovations or repairs.

99. Save all physical copies of necessary paperwork.

Never let the paperwork skip your mind once you finally move into your new home. While cloud-based storage can help you keep tabs on all files, it is a must to keep physical copies of your closing disclosure, deed, mortgage statements, and other documents and store them in a fireproof and locked file cabinet.

100.   Commit to a lifetime of learning.

Buying the house only marks the beginning of homeownership. Think of it as a lifelong learning process. Investing in education as a homeowner can help you ensure that you don't make any costly mistakes so you can make the most out of your first home.

100 Real Estate Seller Tips

1. Install window panes.

If your existing windows are still in tip-top shape, you don't necessarily need to replace them. But you can spruce them up to make them more appealing to buyers. Make your home exude an inviting and friendly appearance by adding wooden or plastic mullions as simple tweaks.

2. Inspect the roof and the gutters.

Your house can easily give off an unkempt look if there are loose downspouts, sagging gutters, or missing shingles on the roof. What's worse is that the flow can even compromise the foundation of the house which can be a very expensive repair.

3. Keep those windows sparkling clean.

Dirt, dust, grime, and all sorts of unwanted particles can find themselves accumulating on your windows. The last thing you want is to make potential buyers turn away because of your grimy windows. Be sure to clean them as often as you can.

4. Curb appeal matters more than anything else.

You want potential buyers to always have a good first impression of your house right from the get-go. After all, first impressions last, especially in the real estate market. Pay closer attention to your property's curb appeal so you can attract more buyers.

5. Bath your house.

If the exterior of your house already looks dirty and grimy, then, don't think twice about renting a gas-powered pressure washer. Rinse away all those years of accumulated dirt by working from top to bottom. This is a job you can do on your own, although you can always hire a professional service if you like.

6. Lay down a stone walkway.

Unlike concrete walkways, a carefully laid-out stone walkway can look so much better. Make sure that your stone walkway will lead your potential buyers all the way to your front door that sports a fresh coat of paint.

7. Adorn your windows with window boxes.

It doesn't matter what type of flowers or plants you choose because window boxes can go a long way to spruce up your house with no need to spend a lot of cash. Window boxes are small updates that can make a big difference in the overall feel of any property.

8. Repaint your house.

If ever your house is no longer sparkling and is starting to look a bit tired and dull, then it is time to give it a much-needed repaint. On the other hand, if you are not ready to commit to repainting the whole house itself, you can settle with touching up just the doors and window frames. You will be surprised by the big difference these simple changes can make.

9. Pay attention to siding replacement.

If the exterior still looks like it can use some fixing and a fresh coat of paint isn't enough, a siding replacement may be necessary. A house that looks and feels great from the outside often sells for a better value at a faster rate.

10. Reseal your driveway.

Does the driveway of your home look like it can use a touchup? Then all you have to do is visit the building supply shop in your area and buy some asphalt. It is an easy and quick fix that can make your driveway look shiny and sparkling all over again.

11. Make your lawn lush and verdant.

Sufficient and proper watering combined with a fast-acting greening fertilizer, such as ammonium sulfate, urea, or ammonium nitrate can make the grass in your lawn or yard look nice and healthy in three weeks' time. Get rid of weeds and trim the edges. These simple acts can make a big difference in your home's overall appeal.

12. Focus on shutter installation.

If your house looks a bit plain and can use something more, try installing shutters in a shade or two darker or lighter. You might want to coordinate the entire color scheme to match the windowpanes and doors. You should also try matching the style of the shutters with that of the house in general.

13. Think of tweaking the front door.

If you have a flat and plain wooden front door, it might be a great thing to consider switching to a raised-panel hardwood door. These doors are now available in different styles and designs with different price ranges that can start as low as $400.

14. Designate a spot for storing your apparel.

Your entryway can quickly feel smaller, cramped, and cluttered if you have too many bags, umbrellas, overcoats, and others kept there. This is something that may turn off potential buyers. It is important for your entryway to feel wider and more welcoming.

15. Spruce up your entryway.

You can make your foyer or entryway stick out even more and capture a buyer's attention with chic wall sconces or overhead lights. You can also embellish the walls with framed mirrors, spot-lit paintings, flowers on the wall table, or other decorative items that are visually stimulating.

16. Use neutral-colored paint in rooms.

As always expected, the most common shade used to make even the smallest spaces feel more spacious is none other than white. Smaller spaces, such as entryways, closets, and bathrooms can easily feel more spacious if you paint them white.

17. Keep all clutter in a rental storage unit.

Any pieces of bulky furniture that make rooms seem cluttered and messy can be easily kept out of the way to improve the feel of your home's overall space.

18. Clean your floors.

Your floors must always be clean and spotless if you want to sell your home fast. Spic-and-span floors can make your entire house appear cleaner, thus making it more enticing to the eyes of potential buyers.

19. Sell off any stuff you no longer want.

Holding a garage sale is a surefire way to eliminate clutter and free your house from any unwanted stuff. To make things even better, you can also earn extra money that you can use to pay for other projects required to help your house sell faster.

20. Keep your walls elegant but simple.

Any wall or room can easily feel crowded and cluttered if there are too many picture frames everywhere you look. Instead, try putting up just one large photo or you can also group the smaller pictures in just one designated space.

21. Get rid of the leaf on your dining table.

Does your dining room table feature a leaf? If yes, then it might be time to remove it and get rid of the extra chairs to make the room feel more spacious.

22. Take advantage of mirrors.

Mirrors can magically expand a room if you strategically place them to reflect anything beautiful, even more so if used in smaller rooms. A good idea here is to use some mirrored backs on the shelves with china pieces or glassware.

23. Put up lights with higher wattage.

Brighter rooms often appear and feel larger than they actually are. If there is any room in your home that is a bit darker and is also smaller than the usual size, putting up higher wattage lighting can do wonders to change the ambiance.

24. Free your home from unwanted smells.

The last thing you want is for your potential buyers to enter your house only to be welcomed by some unwanted odors, whether from your pets or the kitchen. Try to address these smells but avoid using sweet-smelling sprays or potpourris that may still be off-putting to some people.

25. Add a skylight.

Adding a skylight to the hallway, bath, or small kitchen will not just allow light better into the room. At the same time, it can also expand the space while adding a little something extra that will be such a pleasant surprise to potential buyers.

26. Pay attention to your kitchen.

The kitchen is definitely the most commonly used room in most homes today. To make this part of your house stand out more as the focal point, scour it and add as much natural light to the kitchen as possible.

27. Keep the kitchen sealed off from your pets.

Since the kitchen is where you prepare your meals, see to it that there are no signs of pets there. The kitchen must always be free of pet toys, litter boxes, and other signs of your fur babies.

28. Tone down the elements.

When it comes to your kitchen, it might not be wise to invest in elements that are difficult or tricky to change such as flooring or tile. Try toning down the color of the kitchen walls to white to make the room look and feel more simplified.

29. Give your enamel-coated appliances a good refinishing.

If some of your enamel-coated appliances are looking dull, remove the stains using a stiff brush and undiluted bleach. Use auto body polish afterward and finish off with touch-up enamel to hide any unwanted nicks.

30. Refinish other appliances.

Yes, you can also refinish your Coppertone or Avocado appliances. Check online or in the phone book to find companies that refinish tiles because most of them also refinish appliances. Expect to pay around $200 for refinishing every appliance.

31. Light up the work area.

It is a wise idea to install some special lights to brighten up the work areas or surfaces to complement the bright lighting in your kitchen. These dedicated work lights can make moving around the kitchen easier and safer, which can be a bonus to the eyes of potential buyers.

32. Let the bright light outdoors into your kitchen.

Consider getting rid of dark curtains in the kitchen altogether to brighten up this part of the house better. It is also good to use white lace if ever you still prefer your kitchen windows to have some treatments instead of leaving them bare.

33. Clean the bathroom from top to bottom.

As far as the bathroom is concerned, keeping it clean is the most basic and most important rule of thumb you need to follow. See to it that the bathroom is clean starting from the ceiling down to the floor. A bathroom with unwanted musty smells can literally put an end to your hopes of selling your house.

34. Pay attention to the tile and grout.

The tile and grout in the bathroom are prone to dirt and grime accumulation. To keep them clean at all times, you can prepare a water and vinegar solution. If this home remedy doesn't do the trick, you can try switching to a stronger anti-mildew chemical and pair it off with a stiff brush for a deeper clean.

35. Repair tiles with cracks and chips.

Highly noticeable cracked and chipped tiles can easily ruin the look of the entire bathroom. For matching tiles, you can use a knife or screwdriver to take away the damaged tile and the old mortar to prepare the surface for the new tile installation. Once the spot is clean, you can put in the new tile.

36. Re-caulk joints.

A sealant is applied to the joints between the bath and shower and sink. If it seems like this sealant can use a replacement soon, don't waste any minute and replace it right away to make your bathroom sparkle and shine like new all over again.

37. Neutralize any faulty colors.

In case you still have some cartoon characters painted on your pink tiled bathroom wall, this might now be the best time for you to get rid of these rather outdated designs. After all, not all potential buyers will also find these characters as adorable as you do, right?

38. Add a new shower curtain in white.

Just so you know, colored and patterned shower curtains can actually make your bathroom look and feel smaller. To avoid making your bathroom feel cramped, try to put up a new white shower curtain. White shower curtains can make your bathroom look chic and clean at the same time.

39. Polish chrome faucets and fixtures.

Dirty chrome faucets and fixtures never look good and can even make your bathroom look dingy and unkempt. To polish them, avoid using abrasives and use water and vinegar solution. Use this to wipe the chrome pieces clean to bring back their lost shine.

40. Free the sinks from stains.

Stains should never have a place in your bathroom sink. To clean them, prepare a paste made with hydrogen peroxide and cream of tartar to deal with basic stains. For more stubborn stains, use paper towels to line the sink and saturate it with household bleach. Allow the bleach to sit for 30 minutes before wiping the sink clean.

41. Replace or refinish a badly chipped enamel sink.

Replacing or refinishing a badly chipped enamel sink is a job best left to the hands of a professional who can do it on-site. Replacing a sink can often cost you anywhere around $100 to $250 while tubs will obviously cost you more.

42. Fix any leaky faucets.

Leaky bathroom faucets may often give off the impression of neglect to potential homebuyers who will come to visit and view your house for sale. The good news is that fixing leaky faucets is easy, and is something that you can do on your own or entrust to the hands of a pro.

43. Install upgraded faucets, towel rails, and other bathroom fixtures.

Even the simplest upgrade to your bathroom fixtures is already a surefire way to accentuate this part of your home that can give off a great impression among prospective buyers.

44. Get rid of excess stuff and remove any clutter.

Anything not necessary in the bathroom for basic functionality should be kept out of sight. You wouldn't want your potential buyers to see all your stash of unused towels, brushes, and hand creams cluttering the bathroom cabinets.

45. Find a good toilet seat replacement.

A dingy toilet seat isn't the most welcoming sight that potential buyers would want to see the moment they step inside your bathroom. Better replace that old toilet seat and pick something in plain white for added appeal.

46. Secure the wallpaper.

Are there any curling or loose coverings on any wall around the house? All you need is to use some adhesives such as a basic sealer that you can easily find at your local hardware store. Peeling wallpapers are not very pleasing to the eyes, especially if they are already too noticeable.

47. Find a good home for your magazines and books.

A cute basket can be a great place for keeping your magazines and books tidier and more organized. Finding a good home for these reading materials can even create a nice and more welcoming ambiance that potential buyers will surely appreciate.

48. Place potpourri and scented candles around the house.

A house that smells good is always a house that also looks and feels good. Just make sure that instead of heavy-smelling potpourri and scented candles, try to stick with pleasant aromas with light scents and let them waft the air and welcome buyers into your home.

49. Put up some fans.

A well-ventilated house is better than something that feels too suffocating. But if your home has somewhat poor ventilation, your next best option is to install fans that can help circulate the air better around the space.

50. Revamp the living room.

Let your creative juices flow by coming up with ingenious ways to make your living room look more usable while avoiding emphasizing a lot of the furniture pieces you have there.

51. Hide bad views if possible.

Try to keep any view hidden if it is far from appealing. You can command attention by adding a large plant, for example. This is a wiser option instead of covering any flaws with solids or curtains that will only make them more noticeable.

52. Add new treatments for your living room windows.

New window treatments can do wonders to revive your entire living room, not to mention that these are also a great way to show potential buyers that the house has received the tender love, care, and attention it needs and deserves.

53. Cover your old couch or furniture pieces.

It is only normal for your couch and other pieces of furniture to look worn out after all those years of usage. However, potential buyers might not find it pleasant to see those tears on the sofa or scratches on your glass center table. Slipcovers can help hide these flaws easily.

54. Stash your collections somewhere else.

It is never wrong to have a passion for certain things, such as collecting action figures. But instead of letting them out there for buyers to see, you might want to store them somewhere else during your home showings. Some may find your personal belongings and collections a bit cluttered and unappealing.

55. Upgrade the small details.

Upgrading your rails, baseboards, crown moldings, and other parts of your home of this nature can make any space appear nicer than before. What may seem insignificant might just be the very things that a potential homebuyer is looking for.

56. Spend time tending to your wall-to-wall carpet.

Wall-to-wall carpets can add a touch of elegance to any space. However, just like anything else, these can also suffer from wear and tear. If you have this feature in your home, make sure you smooth away any imperfections on it.

57. Eliminate squeaky floors.

Are there some bothersome squeaky floors around the house? The best way to deal with this issue is to apply granite powder to the cracks in the noisy part of the floor. Work this powder into the joints and crevices until the unwanted squeaking stops. You can repeat the process as needed.

58. Perform floor refinishing.

If your floor is already looking like it can use some TLC, you can strip the wax and then re-polish them to bring them back to life. The floors are some of the first things that homebuyers notice, and you wouldn't want to leave them looking soiled.

59. Designate one focal point.

The most common and naturally chosen focal point in many homes is none other than the fireplace. If you already have one, all you have to do is arrange furniture around it. Pianos are also favorite focal points as well as walls of books.

60. Let your dining room area stand out.

The dining room may not be used most often in some homes, but it still needs all the attention you can give. Make the dining room feel more inviting by making it stand out from other parts of the house.

61. Refinish your dining room table and make it sparkle.

The table is often the main focal point of the dining room. You can refinish it to restore its sparkle and ensure that it remains distinct from other furniture pieces.

62. Dress up your dining table.

Your dining table is already charming in and of itself, but you can still accentuate it by buying a new runner or new settings for it. Just a simple dressing-up can go a long way to make your dining table more stunning than ever.

63. Take note of your window décor.

Add some swag to your bare dining room windows to make them more visually interesting. Doing this can instantly brighten up your dining area and make it more inviting where potential homebuyers can envision themselves enjoying meals with their family.

64. Have a centerpiece in place.

No dining room table will ever be complete without a centerpiece. The good news is that you have lots of options to choose from here. Maybe you can use a bowl of fresh fruit or even a soup tureen.

65. Make all rooms look and feel lived in.

A dark and gloomy house that looks like no one has lived in it is never pleasing to the eyes of potential homebuyers. For example, light the ends of the candles in the hallway to make them seem like you are actually using them. You can think of these as props to stage your house in the eyes of prospective buyers.

66. Don't neglect that chandelier.

It is never enough to just have a gorgeous chandelier. What matters more is to dust and clean it. Take note that this lighting fixture serves as the highlight of the whole room, and the last thing you want is for it to be filled with cobwebs and dust.

67. Add a soft touch to the bedrooms.

While most homeowners tend to pay more attention to cleaning the bathroom and kitchen, it is a completely different story as far as the bedrooms are concerned. These areas need to look soft and lived in, to the point that buyers can easily envision themselves sleeping there.

68. Buy new bed linens.

You don't need expensive linens for your bedroom. Some fresh new sheets alone are already a great way to spruce up bedrooms without breaking the bank.

69. Add carpet to the bedroom floors.

The carpeting in your bedrooms is one of the best ways to make anyone feel cozy and comfortable. The soft appearance and feel of carpets can instantly induce comfort and livability.

70. Don't go overboard with the children's rooms.

Those posters in the kid's rooms can easily be taken down. Doing so will let buyers unleash their creativity as they imagine how they will decorate the room.

71. Put away all the kid's toys.

It is all too easy to forget about toys if you have kids around the house, but don't forget that potential home buyers might not have their own children just yet. Avoid turning them off by looking for a neat spot where you can store all those toys.

72. Clear the closets.

Yes, prospective buyers may also want to look inside your closets. Of course, you wouldn't want them to see all the stuff you've amassed through the years, so try making your closets as clean and decluttered as possible.

73. Don't forget that landscaping.

If you think that a wild look is still in, think again. A house that looks like a jungle wouldn't even look enticing to buyers. Be sure to keep that landscape neat and inviting instead of looking like a hurricane destroyed it.

74. Trim away shrubs and hedges.

As some of the most important aspects of your landscaping, shrubs and hedges need your attention, too. While doing so, don't forget to prune any dead branches and limbs. This way, you can let your plants look fresh and healthy.

75. Repair fences and gates that need fixing.

Gates and fences are there for a good reason: they keep the property safe and secure while giving you some privacy. Broken pieces, broken latches, and holes can compromise all these, not to mention that they can also affect aesthetics.

76. Add some gorgeous annuals to your yard.

Flowers in different colors that bloom in season are some of the best additions you can ever have in your yard to make it more appealing than ever.

77. Get new plants.

With the recent rise in the popularity of house plants, you can easily find new varieties that you can add to your landscape. You can choose anything that suits your taste with maintenance requirements that you can keep up with.

78. Turn a plain fence or wall into a work of art.

Ivy, or any type of climbing plant, can effortlessly bring life to what was supposed to be a lifeless and ordinary wall or fence, turning it into a lush work of art.

79. Provide details on pool maintenance.

If your property comes with a pool, buyers might worry about the cost of its upkeep. Make sure you help them understand better that it isn't a bad thing at all. Give them all the details about the cost together with specifications.

80. Offer a detailed year-round description of the garden.

If your seasonal garden is currently not in season, see to it that your potential buyers have a good idea of what the garden goes through at different times of the year.

81. Take landscaping to the next level by planting a full-grown tree.

While trees don't simply grow overnight, it wouldn't cost you that much to hire a professional who can plant and add one to your current landscape.

82. Free your yard of any old and rusty stuff.

Old cars, swing sets, and garden sets that have gathered dust and rust in your yard should be out of it soon. You wouldn't want these things to be there to welcome potential buyers, right?

83. Don't forget to clean the garage and basement.

The garage and basement are two parts of your house that you might not use often. However, these areas still get dirty for some reason. This is why you should never neglect cleaning them before you invite potential buyers over.

84. Get rid of grease and oil stains in the garage.

You can use a commercial degreasing liquid for this particular job. These can lessen, if not completely get rid of, those ugly stains to freshen up your garage and bring it back to life.

85. Eliminate any unnecessary clutter on the garage floor.

Store old, unused things and keep them off the floor. If shelf space is limited in the garage, you can always store them in the attic or even use a temporary storage unit.

86. Give the basement a thorough cleaning.

A well-kempt, clean basement can instantly turn into an appealing extra room in your house. Be sure to use this in your favor to entice more potential buyers.

87. Clean the furnace if your house has one.

A furnace is always a great thing to have in a house, but you need to clean it, too. Wipe it down properly because while this may not be enough to make it look new again, it can still go a long way.

88. Keep your basement clean and safe.

Check the basement for asbestos and other similar harmful things before you invite potential buyers to come and view your house.

89. Always be ready for showings.

You can never tell when a potential buyer will be knocking on your door so make sure you are prepared all the time. Always keep the house clean, and organized, and make sure it smells fresh and pleasant.

90. Establish trust among buyers.

Be professional, discuss things without any doubts or hesitations, and form a win-win ambiance when marketing your home. The moment a buyer senses that you are up to something, expect them to turn around and never look back again.

91. Take your agent's opinion into consideration.

Be sure to look for an agent you can trust and make sure you heed their advice as often as possible. More than anyone else, these professionals know the ins and outs of the industry like the back of their hands.

92. Remove desperation from the equation.

When it comes to selling a house, it is mainly about negotiation. Once you let desperation sweep over you when trying to sell, you might end up with a price that is lower than the actual value of your home. Avoid putting yourself in desperate situations because you obtained more debt than you can handle or you have over-leveraged.

93. First impressions matter the most.

The first impression, most of the time, is the only impression that will last for a long time. Most buyers even decide if they will put an offer on a property in just a matter of seconds so don't miss the chance to make that first impression count.

94. Maintain a positive mindset.

Keeping a positive mindset is a must when trying to sell your house. Your house might be exactly what some buyers are searching for and all you need to do is find them. Use business eyes when selling your property and never take it personally.

95. Refer to the sold comps.

You could get good insights into what buyers are searching for in a house if you refer to the details on recently sold properties. If almost all sold homes have a flower garden, you might want to consider sprucing up your yard with one, too.

96. Say no to over-upgrading.

Make sure every update you make will pay off in the long run and give you the best value for your money. Going overboard with repairs doesn't always increase the value of the property and worse, it may even make you spend more than what it is worth. Consider the competition and try to make your house a bit better than theirs without overdoing it.

97. Use a professional camera.

With the majority of modern home buyers using the internet to check out your house before they actually come to visit in person, the pictures you use play a crucial role in the listing process. Don't miss out on the chance to use them in your favor. Buy or rent a high-quality DSLR camera complete with a wide-angle lens when taking snaps of your home.

98. Make the deal sweeter.

Add some incentives to buyers who give their offers. Even the simplest perks can make some people more inclined to purchase a house.

99. Visit the open houses in the area.

Visiting the open houses in the neighborhood can educate you on the things you should and shouldn't do when marketing your property. This can increase your chances of closing the deal sooner than later.

100.   Put yourself in the buyer's shoes.

Search online first for local houses that are the same as your property. Check how they present their houses and how they price them. What features stand out the most to you? Which ones turn you off? Note your own reactions to each listing and make some adjustments to your own accordingly.

100 Real Estate Terms

1. Acceleration Clause

An acceleration clause is the contract provision that permits lenders to require borrowers to repay the entire outstanding loan when a breach of contract occurs or if payments are not being made.

2. Accretion

Accretion refers to the slow process of acquisition or growth of land, usually when a natural action of water deposits soil. Most of the time, long-term accretion can even increase the total size of a property.

3. ARM

ARM, or the adjustable-rate mortgage, comes with a flexible interest rate. These adjustable-rate mortgages have a fixed period and during this, the initial interest rate will stay the same. After this period, the interest rate will adjust at a pre-set frequency. This fixed-rate period varies anywhere around a month up to 10 years.

4. Agreement of Sale

The agreement of sale is the form that indicates that the buyer agrees to buy a property while the seller also consents to sell said property with the specific terms and conditions that have been illustrated in from the two parties involved.

5. Alienation

Alienation refers to the act of transferring ownership, title, interest in real estate, or an estate to another party from another.

6. Antitrust Laws

Antitrust laws are the collection of both state and federal government laws that are responsible for regulating the organization and conduct of business corporations, typically to encourage a fair competition that will work to the consumers' advantage.

7. Appraisal Contingency

Many banks and big lenders today require buyers to conduct an appraisal on the property before they grant a loan. They do this to ensure that the value of the property will be somewhat close to the value of the offer that has been accepted.

8. Appraiser

Even though agents and brokers often have some idea of the process of valuation, most of the time, they work with an appraiser who can do this job on their behalf. All appraisers are expected to have comprehensive knowledge of the different valuation methods. Most states today also require a particular certification or license to carry out these duties.

9. Appurtenance

The term "appurtenance" is a noun that describes a particular item that is connected to something. As far as real estate is concerned, it can already be called an appurtenance after something has been installed on a certain property. This means that this will be passed on to the new owner once the property has been sold off.

10. Arbitration

Arbitration refers to the method to resolve disputes. Real estate arbitration typically takes place if two homeowners want to address a concern and don't want the courts to have any direct involvement with the issue.

11. As-Is

Any property that is marketed in an "as-is" condition often implies that the seller is not willing to perform all or most of the repairs required. This can also mean that the property is priced as-is which is often lower compared to the pricing in the current market of the area.

12. Attorney-in-Fact

An attorney-in-fact is someone who is given the authority to act on another person's behalf, usually in business or for any form of transaction in a business.

13. Avulsion

Avulsion refers to the immediate action wherein land is torn away or added by violent acts from different natural causes. A hurricane or a broken dam is a good example of avulsion.

14. Bilateral Contract

A bilateral contract is an agreement between groups or between at least two people. Many personal and business contracts fall into this particular category.

15. Blockbusting

Blockbusting refers to the illegal practice in which real estate agents sell properties at a cheap price to a certain race and then sell those same properties to a minority at a much higher price.

16. Buffer Zone

Buffer zones refer to the spaces of land amid two used districts, such as a highway, playground, or park. The main purpose of these buffer zones is to ease and simplify the transition from one zone to another.

17. Bundle of Rights

The moment a person buys a property, that person will then get the rights to said property. Said rights can then be divided and distributed to various parties.

18. Buyer's Agent

A buyer's agent is a professional that you enlist if you are someone who is in the market hoping to find and purchase a new house. Your buyer's agent will be the one to represent you during the transaction and they will receive a fee in exchange for the services they offer.

19. Buyer's Home Sale Contingency

A buyer's home sale contingency is a contingency that gives the buyer permission to have the contract canceled if ever they fail to sell off their current house within a specific period of time.

20. Caveat Emptor

The Latin phrase *"caveat emptor"* means "Let the buyer beware." This concept states that it is the responsibility of the buyer to check the quality of a particular product before the actual buying process ensues.

21. Closing

Closing refers to the last step in the execution of a transaction in real estate. This is the time when the official payment and ownership will be transferred to the rightful parties. This step often takes place once a purchase agreement has been made and it is now possible to transfer the title of the property.

22. Closing Costs

Closing costs refer to the assortment of fees that include the fees being charged by the lender, attorneys, the title company, taxing authorities, insurance companies, real estate agents, homeowner's associations, as well as other companies related to the closing settlement. The closing costs are often paid off during a real estate transaction's closing.

23. Co-op

A co-op refers to a nonprofit organization that is complete with its own set of board of directors. Every resident is also considered a shareholder. A co-op and a condominium are distinct from each other because a majority of co-op associations require that a committee made up of existing co-op owners give their approval to a potential buyer.

24. Co-ownership

Co-ownership is when two or more individuals hold the title to a single parcel of real estate. These parties are then referred to as concurrent owners or co-owners. Individuals may become co-owners of properties as joint tenants, tenants in common, tenants by community property, or tenants by the entirety.

25. Condemnation

Condemnation is the procedure that a private or public entity uses with the powers granted from the eminent domain to take real estate under private ownership.

26. Condominium

Popularly known for its shortened version, condo, a condominium is a specific type of living that resembles an apartment. The only difference is that each condo can be sold off independently, which is why every condominium is considered a form of real estate.

27. Constructive Eviction

The term "constructive eviction" is used in real property law used for describing a circumstance wherein a landlord either fails to do something or does something that they have the legal duty to render.

28. Contingent Property

Contingent property is the term used during the acceptance of an offer for a property but there is a contingency or a condition that is stated in the contract. This contingency should then be met before the sale of the property can be pushed through.

29. Corporation

A corporation can be formed either for nonprofit or profit purposes. A board of directors is responsible for the management and operation of a corporation. Every corporation has a specific set of liabilities, privileges, and rights beyond those that exist in partnerships. There are pros and cons associated with doing business as a corporation.

30. Cost Approach

The cost approach is the method of appraisal in real estate that indicates that the price the buyer will pay for the property must be equal to the cost of constructing an equivalent building on the specific property in question.

31. Counteroffer

A counteroffer and a purchase agreement are essentially similar. Once a counteroffer has been made, it will then put an end to the existence of the original offer since the seller has already legally rejected it.

32. Days on Market (DOM)

Days on market refers to the number of days from the specific date when the property has been listed for sale on the multiple listing service or MLS of the local real estate brokers up to the date when the seller has signed a contract with the buyer for the sale of the property.

33. Debt-to-Income Ratio

DTI, or debt-to-income ratio, refers to the number that mortgage lenders use. This is determined by your overall debt expenses in addition to your housing payment per month. The total sum is divided by your gross income per month and then multiplied by 100. It helps lenders gauge affordability according to their available loan programs and lets them estimate the amount you can afford to pay for a mortgage every month.

34. Deed

A deed refers to the written legal document that conveys the ownership of a real estate property to another property from another.

35. Deed Restrictions

The deed restrictions state the limitations to the use of a certain property imposed either by a current or past owner and most of the time, these are often legally bound for life.

36. Defeasance Clause

A defeasance clause is the required contract provision that guarantees that the title of the property will be transferred to the buyer after the full payment of the mortgage.

37. Due Diligence

The purchase agreement might indicate the due diligence period of time or the time frame that a buyer is given to completely assess a property. Experts are often hired to conduct an inspection of the property, carry out tests, and others to help the buyer decide how to go about the rest of the process.

38. Earnest Money Deposit or EMD

An EMD, or earnest money deposit, also sometimes called a "good faith" deposit, refers to the initial funds a buyer is required to put down after the seller accepts the offer of the buyer. This shows that the buyer is not only serious about the purchase but is also willing to spend their money.

The earnest money deposit amount can vary between 1% to 5% of the property's sales price. An escrow company often holds the EMD or as otherwise provided for under the PSA or purchase and sale agreement.

39. Equity

Equity refers to the investment that homeowners have in their homes. Equity is calculated by taking the home's market value and subtracting any liens or mortgages against the property. The remaining amount is considered the equity that you have in your property.

Building equity is necessary since homeowners can use this financial asset for obtaining loans that can be used for financing items like home repairs or paying off debts with higher interest.

40. Erosion

Erosion is the opposite of accretion and refers to the wearing away of the soil or land by the action of water, wind, ice, currents, or other forces of nature. The size of a property may decrease as a result of long-term erosion.

41. Errors and Omissions Insurance

This is a form of insurance that is required in some but not all states. This is a specific type of liability insurance that offers professionals protection against claims of negligent actions or inadequate work.

42. Escheat

The ownership of the property will revert to the government if the owner of the property passes away without leaving behind any properly documented plan for its inheritance. Escheat ensures that the property will have ownership at all times.

43. Escrow

Escrow refers to the way of transferring property and money from one party to another with the help of a neutral third-party agent, also called an escrow agent. Thanks to escrow, it is safer for sellers and buyers alike to close the sale with no need to worry that they will be cheated or snubbed.

44. Escrow Holder

An escrow holder is an agent and depositary or impartial third party that will collect the money, personal property, documents, instruments, or other valuable things that will be held until the specified happens or the described conditions are performed, typically outlined in written mutual instructions from all parties involved.

45. Estate at Will

When you speak of an estate at will, it means that it is possible to end it at any given time. This estate basically has an indefinite term. It is also important to take note that an estate of will is not recognized in all states and those that do may have different laws in place.

46. Exclusive Right to Sell Listing

A specific broker is dedicated as the only agent who will work with the seller and will also have exclusive authorization for representing the property in question. A commission will be given to the broker regardless of who will sell off the property during the duration of the listing agreement.

47. Express Contract

Express contracts take place if the two parties involved legally form an agency relationship. This means that they will sit down and write a contract that states their relationship. It is the most common way to create agency relationships.

48. Fannie Mae

Fannie Mae, or the Federal National Mortgage Association, purchases mortgages on the secondary market and puts all of them together. The association will then sell them back to the open market investors in the form of mortgage securities bonds.

49.Fee Simple Absolute

Simply called "fee simple," this term refers to an estate in land. This is the highest form of ownership of real estate that the law recognizes wherein the owner can enjoy the fullest potential of a property and is limited only by the powers of the government.

50.FHA Loans

FHA loans belong to the group of loans under the insurance of the federal government. It means that rather than actually lending cash, the FHA ensures private lenders and banks that they are going to cover losses that might take place if ever the borrower fails to have a timely or full repayment of the loan.

51.FHA 230k Rehab Loan

The FHA 230k Rehab Loan is the fixer-upper loan that blends the mortgage loan together with a loan that will help in the repayment of updates or repairs such as energy-related updates or structural repairs. This is not meant to lend based on luxury upgrades, like adding tennis courts or swimming pools.

52.Fixed Rate Mortgage

A fixed-rate mortgage means that your interest rate will remain the same throughout the loan's entire duration. These mortgages are usually available as loans good for 30, 20, 15, or 10 years. The most popular and common types of home loans so far are those that last for 15 and 30 years and these account for most of the residential mortgages today.

53. Freehold Estate

Freehold estate refers to an estate wherein you will have the exclusive right of enjoying an indefinite possession of a particular property. This is the direct opposite of a leasehold estate in which the possession is limited by a certain period of time.

54. General Agent

General agents are the agents hired who can carry out all of the acts related to a specific business that the principal has designated the agent to. This kind of relationship is continuous most of the time.

55. General Warranty Deed

A general warranty deed is a deed where the seller or grantor guarantees that they hold clear title to a parcel of real estate with the right of selling it to the buyer or grantee.

56. Gross Lease

The gross lease is the rental agreement for using the property in which the tenant will pay a set amount that doesn't change as the result of alterations in the different expenses of the property.

57. Gross Rent Multiplier

The gross rent multiplier is the ratio of a real estate investment's price to its yearly rental income before accounting for different expenses like utilities, insurance, and property taxes. To be more specific, this is the measure of an investment property's value which is obtained by dividing the sale price of the property by its gross annual rental income.

58. Hard Money Loan

A hard money loan is a method of borrowing without the help of traditional lenders. A hard money lender finances the loan depending on the said property and not on the credit score you have. It often requires a significant down payment as well as a short repayment schedule.

59. Home Inspection

The home inspection refers to the examination of the real estate property and its condition. It often takes place in connection with the sale of the property. The buyer hires a licensed professional inspector to visit the property and come up with a report regarding its condition and necessary repairs. This is usually part of the due diligence period to help buyers fully assess whether they wish to purchase a specific property as-is or request the seller to either pay for or complete certain repairs.

60. Homeowner's Association

A homeowner's association or HOA is the private association responsible for managing a condominium or planned community. Once you buy an HOA-managed property, you also agree to follow the rules of the HOA and pay its annual or monthly HOA dues. If you don't comply or pay, the HOA usually can file to foreclose on the property or a lien against that property.

61. Homeowner's Insurance

A homeowner's insurance is a type of property insurance that offers coverage for damages and losses. This insurance covers the house of an individual together with the assets found inside the property. This may also offer liability coverage against accidents on the property or in the home.

62. Home Sale Contingency

Home sale contingency is for the buyer to inform the seller that one part of their condition to buy the property of the seller relies on the ability of the buyer to finalize a close on the current property. It is often negotiated with an addendum to a contract or a clause in the contract.

63. Inspection Contingency

The inspection contingency or also called due diligence contingency is the clause often offered in the purchase agreement that will grant the buyer a preset amount of time during escrow to carry out any inspections if and when necessary.

64. Joint Tenancy

If there are joint tenants who own a certain property, the interest of the deceased owner will automatically get transferred to the rest of the surviving owners.

65. Land Lease

When you buy a house, you will traditionally own the house as well as the land on which the property has been built. Some instances may involve a land lease, and this means that the home will be under your ownership while you pay rent to the owner of the land.

66. Leasehold Estate

A leasehold estate or also called a less than freehold estate is a type of estate that is held by the one who leases or rents the property. The limitation of time is the main difference between a freehold estate and a leasehold estate. Since a lease is a form of legal estate, it is possible to buy and sell leasehold estates on the open markets.

67. Lender

Lenders can be a private or public group or an individual. Financial institutions such as banks can lend available funds to another person. The lender is often whom people turn to to get the loans they need.

68. Lien

Liens are a form of security interest granted over the item for securing the payment of debts or performance of other obligations. A lien will serve to ensure an underlying obligation. This obligation is often paying the loan back.

69. Life Estate

A life estate is the interest in a real estate property that is held throughout the lifetime of the designated person. This might be limited by the lifespan of the person who holds it or by the life of someone else. The designated person is referred to as the life tenant.

70. Loan

A loan refers to the amount of money used for a property that is expected to be paid back together with interest. To buy property, many people use some kind of loan. Mortgages, car loans, and student loans are some of the most common types of loans you can encounter today.

71. Loan Contingency

The loan contingency, also called mortgage contingency, is the addendum or clause in the offer contract that lets the buyer back out of the deal and retain their deposit if they fail to secure a mortgage with the specific terms throughout a fixed time period.

72. Lot and Block

Lot and block is a method of appraisal specifically used for areas with a dense population such as suburbs and metropolitan areas. This begins with an expansive tract of land that is already described by a different form of survey system. The entire area will then be divided into smaller lots with a map created as a result.

73. Material Defect

Material defects are issues with the property or any part of it that would have a substantial effect on the property's overall value or that involves significant risk to those people who are living on the land.

74. Mortgage Lien

The mortgage lien is a type of specific voluntary lien. This is actually the most common form of voluntary real estate lien. The moment you borrow money to purchase a real estate property, you will give a lender a lien against that property. It is also known as a deed of trust lien in some states.

75. Mortgage Pre-Approval Letter

It is important to get a mortgage pre-approval letter since this will give the buyer a good idea of how much they can afford. Lenders issue this letter that identifies the type of loan, amount of loan, and the terms that the buyer will qualify for after checking the debt-to-income ratios of the buyer together with the credit history and cash on hand.

76. Multiple Listing Service

The multiple listing service or MLS is the database that lets its members, including brokers and real estate agents, add and access information regarding the for-sale properties in an area. Once a property has been listed for sale, a listing agent will log it into the local MLS. Agents of buyers usually check the MLS to stay updated on what is available in the current market together with the prices of similar homes for sale.

77. Natural Hazards Disclosure Report

A natural hazards disclosure or NHD is a report that most states require that discloses if the property located in a certain area has higher natural hazard risks. The seller often pays for this report and the buyer receives it during escrow. An NHD report covers natural hazard zones such as special flood hazard areas, earthquake fault zones, very high fire hazard severity zones, potential flooding areas, and more.

78. Net Listing

The net listing is when the agent agrees in selling the property of the owner for a determined minimum price. Anything that is more than this minimum price will belong to the agent as a form of commission.

79. Offer or Counteroffer

The buyer makes a formal offer on the property they wish to buy. The offer can be a total list price or what is considered a fair market value by you and your agent. The seller may accept the offer right away or make a counteroffer.

80. Pending Property

Pending is the term that indicates the acceptance of the offer, and the two parties will move forward and proceed with the sale. If the property is still pending, this is still in the period after resolving all of the contingencies.

81. Periodic Tenancy

The periodic tenancy refers to the leasehold agreement that states the initial tenancy period together with the agreement's length. However, it doesn't end after the set period. It is a type of leasehold agreement that is automatically renewed.

82. Pre-approval

To get pre-approved, homebuyers are required to fill out the application that lets a lender identify their financial situation, such as their creditworthiness, ability to repay, or debt-to-income ratio. Once it is available, the lender can give a letter to the buyer that states the specific amount of loan that they were pre-approved for together with the overall sales price they are approved for.

83. Preliminary Report

The preliminary report shows any problems with a title that the seller must deal with to render a clear title. This report gives information such as easements, liens, and history of ownership. The title company will gather the report by looking for the existing records of the property at the office of the county recorder.

84. Pre-qualification

Pre-qualification is the amount estimated by the lender that a homebuyer can expect to get approved for throughout the loan process. To get pre-qualified, the lender will quickly assess the financial situation of the buyer based only on what the buyer informs the lender and not based on any verifications or proof.

85. Price Fixing

Fixing refers to the practice of putting a price on a service or good to make a specific price a standard. Even if it is only implied, an agreement with the rest of the brokerages to set a standard rate of commission is a violation of antitrust laws.

86. Principal

The principal or client is the party who has already signed an agreement with the agent or a broker in particular. Simply put, the principal is any person who has direct involvement in a contract, like a seller or a buyer.

87. Probate Sale

Probate sales take place if the homeowner passes away without leaving the property to someone or writing a will. In cases like this, the probate court will give authority to the estate attorney or other similar representatives to employ a real estate agent who will be in charge of selling the property.

88. Property Manager

Property managers are people who are hired to manage and maintain a property. The property manager can make the life of a landlord much easier in many ways. These professionals can handle everyday tasks such as maintaining the property, collecting rent, or dealing with new tenants.

89. Property Tax

Property tax is a type of real estate ad-valorem tax. The local government calculates this tax that is paid by the property's owner. The tax is often based on the owned property's total value.

90. Purchase Agreement

The purchase agreement is the contract that will legally bind two or several parties together to certain obligations. This agreement creates a legally binding contract between the seller and the buyer.

91. Real Estate Broker

Real estate brokers are people who serve as an intermediary between buyers and sellers of a real estate property. Brokers can work on their own or hire other agents. The main difference between a real estate agent and a broker is that brokers can work on their own while agents are required to work under the supervision of licensed brokers. A standard license is separate from a broker's license.

92. Real-estate Owned

Real-estate owned, or REO, is the designation rendered to properties that a lender owns because of a failed foreclosure sale at an auction. An REO property can often give the buyer a chance to be bought for a value below the market since most banks prefer reinvesting the proceeds instead of wasting time on an extended period of marketing the property.

93. Rent-back

Rent-back, also called leaseback, pertains to an arrangement where the buyer, who is the new homeowner at the moment, will agree to let the seller, who is the now-tenant, remain in the property beyond the close of escrow. Terms are negotiated before the situation happens and usually involve a lease deposit, a length of time allowable, and a daily rental rate.

94. Short Sale

The property in a short sale is often being sold for lower than the debt that the property has secured. Short sales require the approval of the lender of the seller since the sale's proceeds will only be short of the owed amount. Many lenders have drawn out a long approval process for short sales which requires more time to close compared to traditional sales.

95. Tenancy in Common

Two or several tenants own a parcel of real estate in the case of tenancy in common. When a tenant in common passes away, his or her share will then be transferred to the heir or estate of the deceased tenant.

96. Tenants by the Entirety

Some states use tenants by the entirety as a special kind of co-ownership that allow a wife or husband to inherit the ownership interest of the other spouse upon death. A couple that is a tenant by the entirety will automatically have the right of survivorship. Once the other spouse passes away, the surviving spouse will immediately become the property's sole owner.

97. Title Contingency

If the property title is still under review, the buyer can have a title contingency added to the offer. A title report will then be made during this process, which may disclose a conflicting status of ownership in which the buyer can choose to back out of the sale.

98. Title Search

The title search checks the public records for the property's history including purchases, sales, tax, and other types of liens. A title examiner generally conducts a search with the use of title plants and often the country records to examine who has been listed as the property's record owner.

99. Trust Sale

Trust sales mean that the property will be sold by the trustee of the living trust instead of a private party. Most of the time, it is because the original owner of the property already died or their assets have been placed in a living trust.

100. VA Loan

VA loans are mortgage loans made available for members of the military service, eligible surviving spouses, and veterans. These loans usually come with much better terms compared to traditional mortgages, which makes them popularly sought after.

25 Real Estate Q&A

15 Buyer Q & A

1. Is a seller required to accept my offer if it is higher than the list price?

No, sellers are not required to accept offers even if these are more than the list price.

2. Do I need a realtor when buying a house?

It is strongly recommended to have a realtor when buying a house. Realtors can make the entire home buying process easier and more convenient for you as a buyer.

3. What should I do first if I want to buy a house?

Getting approved for a mortgage is the absolute first step you need to take if you are planning to buy a house. It will be somewhat difficult or even impossible to buy a new house if you don't get approved for a mortgage.

4. What is earnest money?

Earnest money is like the deposit you give if you want to rent a place. This is made in good faith to show to the seller that the offer of the buyer is legitimate. This amount is often 1% to 2% of the property's selling price.

5. How does earnest money deposit work?

The amount of the deposited earnest money is deducted from the final price that the buyer will pay at the closing table. Most of the time, when the deposit is larger, the purchase offer will also look stronger to the seller.

6. Is there a specific number of houses to view first before buying one?

The specific number of houses you view depends on many factors. The good news is that today, you can easily view houses online by browsing detailed photographs or taking virtual tours so you can view as many houses as you want.

7. How much should be my offer to sellers?

You are the only one who will be able to determine how much your offer should be. While you can always seek advice from your realtor, at the end of the day, you are the only person who can decide on the amount of your offer to sellers.

8. Is buying a house better than renting one?

Buying a house is a solid investment but for some people, renting is also a better choice depending on the situation. But when the interest rates are extremely low, paying a mortgage might be cheaper than paying rent.

9. Is a final walk-through required?

It is not required to do a final walk-through, but it is still highly recommended. A final walk-through can give you a better chance to ensure and check that nothing changed since your previous visits or initial inspection.

10. Is a home inspection necessary?

Yes, you can order a home inspection yourself or you can ask your realtor to do it for you. Home inspections are among the most important steps when buying any property. Professional inspectors can confirm if the house is cared for properly and can also determine its value.

11. Should I sell my current house before I buy a new one?

It will largely depend on your funds and your ability to look for temporary housing. It might be best to sell your current house before you buy a new one if you need more equity to meet a mortgage plan or purchase your new home.

12. What will happen if I back out of purchasing a house?

It is okay if your get cold feet about buying a house. It is normal to have second thoughts or even choose a completely different direction than what you originally planned. You can also forfeit your earnest money if you back out of the purchase.

13. How does a mortgage work?

A mortgage is a form of loan for financing a property. It serves as a secure loan with a fixed interest rate and can be paid off within 30 or 15 years. This can come in handy for buyers who don't have enough funds to pay for a property's price in full cash.

14. How does an escrow entail work?

The term escrow to the hired neutral third party that handles the property transaction, exchange of money, and all relevant documents. It holds the documents and money in a trust until the sale's terms and conditions are all met and satisfied.

15. Who will pay the realtor fees during a home purchase?

While there is no guarantee, most of the time, the seller is the one who is responsible for paying the realtor fees, making it more sensible to work with one if you are the buyer.

10 Seller Q & A

16. Do I need to put up a For Sale sign in my yard?

No, you don't need to install the For Sale sign in your yard or lawn. But it will be in your best interest to let your realtor do so to ensure maximum exposure of your property so you can sell it for the highest possible price.

17. Are prices negotiable in real estate?

Yes, almost everything is negotiable in real estate. There is often a difference between the list price of your house and how much you actually sell it for. The saturation of the current market determines the amount of available wiggle room for negotiation.

18. How long will it take to sell my property?

It may take around 4 to 6 weeks to sell a house once it is on the market. But in a fairly hot market, you can even expect to have your house off the market in just a matter of a week.

19. What should I do to prepare my house for sale?

First impressions are especially important in real estate. Clean and declutter all rooms and check for and repair any damage. Make sure the electrical system, plumbing, and HVAC are all working properly.

20. Why is the assessed value of my home different from its market value?

A property's assessed value is given by a public tax assessor and is typically done annually for taxation purposes. Fair market value, on the other hand, is the price of the property that the seller and willing buyer have agreed upon.

21.Do I need to stage my house before I list it for sale?

It depends on the condition of your property and the current local market. If your house is in good condition overall and the current market is a seller's market with higher demand than the available supply, it may no longer be necessary to stage your house.

22.Should I have a home inspection ordered?

It is never a bad idea to have your home inspected before selling it, especially if you want to get the best price. Since most homebuyers prefer properties that underwent a home inspection, you might as well order one.

23.What options do I have if I don't sell my house?

You have several options if your house doesn't sell. You can leave it on the market at its current list price, increase or reduce the list price depending on the circumstances, or cancel the listing and re-list it at a later date.

24.What is a real estate commission fee?

The seller pays the agent via commission in real estate transactions. This is 5% to 6% of the final sale price of the property. Most of the time, the seller's agent and the buyer's agent have a 50/50 split of the total commission fee.

25. What affects a property's selling price?

Multiple factors can affect the selling price of a property. Some of these are the prices of similar-sized properties and the neighborhood where it is located. The condition and age of the house and the need for repairs also influence the selling price.

40 Real Estate Quotes for Social Media

1. Ninety percent of all millionaires become so through owning real estate. More money has been made in real estate than in all industrial investments combined. The wise young man or wage earner of today invests his money in real estate.- Andrew Carnegie.

2. Buy land. They're not making it anymore. - Mark Twain

3. The rich buy assets. The poor have expenses. The middle class buys liabilities they think are assets. The poor and the middle-class work for money. The rich have money to work for them. - Robert Kiyosaki.

4. Never depend on a single income. Make investments to create a second source. - Warren Buffet.

5. Wealth is the transfer of money from the impatient to the patient. - Warren Buffet.

6. Price is what you pay. Value is what you get. - Warren Buffet.

7. Risk comes from love knowing what you're doing. - Warren Buffett.

8. The best investment on Earth is earth - Louis Glickman,

9. Don't wait to buy real estate; buy real estate and wait. - T. Harv Eker.

10. Find out where the people are going and buy the land before they get there." - William Penn Adair.

11. The major fortunes in America have been made in land. - John D. Rockefeller

12. He is not a full man who does not own a piece of land. - Hebrew Proverb

13. Everyone wants a piece of land. It's the only sure investment. It can never depreciate like a car or washing machine. Land will only double its value in ten years. - Sam Shepard

14. But land is land, and it's safer than the stocks and bonds of Wall Street swindlers. - Eugene O'Neill

15. Buy on the fringe and wait. Buy land near a growing city! Buy real estate when other people want to sell. Hold what you buy! - John Jacob Astor

16. A funny thing happens in real estate. When it comes back, it comes back up like gangbusters. - Barbara Corcoran

17. Real estate is an imperishable asset, ever-increasing in value. It is the most solid security that human ingenuity has devised. It is the basis of all security and about the only indestructible security. - Russell Sage

18. What we call real estate - the solid ground to build a house on - is the broad foundation on which nearly all the guilt of this world rests. - Nathaniel Hawthorne

19. Owning a home is a keystone of wealth... both financial affluence and emotional security. - Suze Orman

20. I have always liked real estate; farmland, pastureland, timberland, and city property. I have had experience with all of them. I guess I just naturally like 'the good Earth,' the foundation of all our wealth. - Jesse Jones

21. Now, one thing I tell everyone is to learn about real estate. Repeat after me: real estate provides the highest returns, the greatest values, and the least risk. - Armstrong Williams

22. Real estate cannot be lost or stolen, nor can it be carried away. Purchased with common sense, paid for in full, and managed with reasonable care, it is about the safest investment in the world. - Franklin D. Roosevelt

23. The house you looked at today and wanted to think about until tomorrow may be the same house someone looked at yesterday and will buy today. - Koki Adasi

24. Buy real estate in areas where the path exists…and buy more real estate where there is no path, but you can create your own. - David Waronker

25. It is a comfortable feeling to know that you stand on your own ground. Land is about the only thing that can't fly away. - Anthony Trollope

26. The land is the only thing in the world worth working for, worth fighting for, worth dying for because it's the only thing that lasts. - Margaret Mitchell

27. Real estate investing, even on a very small scale, remains a tried and true means of building an individual's cash flow and wealth. - Robert Kiyosaki

28. Buying real estate is not only the best way, the quickest way, the safest way, but the only way to become wealthy. - Marshall Field

29. Every person who invests in well-selected real estate in a growing section of a prosperous community adopts the surest and safest method of becoming independent, for real estate is the basis of wealth. - Theodore Roosevelt

30. Landlords grow rich in their sleep. - John Stuart Mill

31. The problem with real estate is that it's local. You have to understand the local market. -Robert Kiyosaki

32. I will forever believe that buying a home is a great investment. Why? Because you can't live in a stock certificate. You can't live in a mutual fund.-Oprah Winfrey

33. Home is the nicest word there is.-Laura Ingalls Wilder,

34. You are not buying a house; you are buying a lifestyle.

35. Buying a house won't bring you happiness, but turning it into a home certainly will.

36. There is something permanent and something extremely profound in owning a home.

37. To purchase a home is to subconsciously gain the respect of many in your community.

38. The best time to plant a tree is 20 years ago. The second best time is now. — Chinese Proverb

39. YOLO = You Only List Once ... when you list with me!

40. I need your listing; I already sold all of mine.

PART 2- SOCIAL MEDIA MARKETING TIPS

Social Media is powerful. Because people use social media almost daily, they use it on their cell phones and laptops. With social media, you can easily connect with anyone around your local area cheaply and affordable.

And the keys to successful social media marketing are creating engaging content, connecting with your audience, and, most importantly, sharing your personal story and life.

For many years, I made one big mistake: I only used social media to run ads and promote my business, but I never mentioned my life and personal story.

I have been timid and introverted since I was young, and I am not comfortable with social media. If you go to my profile, you will notice I rarely update it; when I was 10, my teacher asked me to share a story for 10 minutes; I was scared to death. I eventually stood on the platform quietly for 10 minutes -It was embarrassing.

Even though I overcame much of my shyness as I grew up, social media is still something I don't feel comfortable using, and I did not use them.

A few years ago, I started my digital marketing agency; I struggled to get a client, even though it's easy for me to sell a $97 product online. I cannot sell my service.

I was frustrated, but I was not ready to quit; I decided to study those who crushed it online, became a student of a few 8-figures entrepreneurs, and reverse engineer their marketing method.

I noticed they have one thing in common - they all have a solid personal brand, and they all share about themselves on social media.

I decided to model what they did and include social media marketing in my business. So I started sharing my story on social media. I even bought ads to promote my post; after a few months, I closed my first high-ticket clients.

The power of social media is not only in its reach but also in its ability to connect.

For someone to buy from you, they need to know you, like you, and trust you. And social media make it an excellent place for someone to get to know you. Personally.

In this chapter, I will share some tips for growing your business using social media profile, and in the "information" chapter, I will share more about content creation with you.

Tips To Do Social Media Marketing

Here are some best social media marketing tips that you can apply without having experience or proper knowledge. Just read the article carefully, and you will know how you can get more leads from social media.

1. Keep Content Responsive

The common mistake of most realtors is that they still think people use laptops or PCs to do their important work or search for anything.

They should know that time has changed and the majority of people switch to mobile phones to do major work.

Especially google searches. Mobile phones are portable and stay in the pockets of everyone.

That's why they do not need to sit in a proper place to open the laptop and use the internet.

They have the facility to use mobiles anywhere and anytime. Due to this portability, they prefer mobile phones.

Google will show your name if you use marketing tools in the right way and have a registered brand on google maps.

But if the site architecture is not compatible with mobile, then the patient cannot navigate to the proper information and move to other realtors.

So make a website according to mobile architecture too. You can link your website to different social media platforms and easily view the content with a responsive architecture.

2. Consider Social Media Messaging:

It is important to communicate with the prospects to know their needs and what they expect from you. Many realtors just use social media marketing to upload posts.

They do not check the message and read the comments, which is not a good thing. Many social media apps allow you to have effective communication with prospects.

The major apps for just communication purposes are WhatsApp, Telegram, Messenger, and Viber.

If you do not want to use different platforms for posting content and communication, stick to the ones you currently use.

You can chat with your prospects through Instagram and Facebook as well. Without making any assumptions, try to listen to what prospects say and resolve their problems.

3. Make Videos:

Most realtors feel shy to communicate with their followers on social media platforms. This can become a barrier to the promotion of the brand.

But do not worry; social media has a solution for all the problems.

Social media gives the facility to upload content in the form of video. Real estate agents who feel just record the important information that they want to deliver and post it on social media.

In general, you can post videos on any social platform. But there is a specific platform called YouTube. Here you can just share videos related to your work and get reviews from clients.

YouTube is the best social media marketing platform as most people spend their time watching different entertainment videos.

You can have more organic leads by delivering a message in the form of video rather than text.

4. Go Live:

After the video going live is the best option to promote the services. It is just like the video call but with your followers.

They have the option to write a message, and you can answer them by speaking.

Facebook and Instagram focus on making this technology better. They allow different ads to pop up during live chat so that interested prospects can directly go to the page.

In the live video, you can show people your workplace and the equipment that you use.

Moreover, you can ask people for reviews. So that you can make changes if people have any complaints about your work and services.

5. Invest In Social Media Ads

Social media ads work just like google ads, but the platform is different. Google ads display on the google search result pages while social media ads display as a post.

During your regular scrolling, you can see the video that is labeled with the ad. No matter whether you follow the page or not, you will see the ad.

It is because the social media marketing. Invest your money in selecting the social media packages to increase the reach of your posts to a high level.

6. Stay Professional:

Professionalism matters a lot in every profession. If you use social media, you know that every social media platform has a different tone. Also, they have different privacy policies.

The type of content you see on Facebook is different from Instagram. But still, there are many similarities between them.

But if we talked about LinkedIn, then it is a completely different platform in terms of professionalism.

Most people use this platform especially to promote their services. There are fewer chances that people have fake accounts and waste your time by sending you irrelevant messages.

Here you can represent your brand as a professional real estate agent. Be sure about the words you use between the communication as it represents a person's personality.

7. Post high quality & viral content

Content marketing continues to be king in the world of digital marketing. This means that you need always to be able to post high-quality content if you want to be successful with your social media efforts.

The biggest problem that marketers face when it comes to their social media engagement is that they simply don't have the time to run every aspect of their business and come up with quality content that can go viral with ease.

Time is an essential part of any successful strategy in social media, but unfortunately, it's impossible for someone to handle everything by themselves and still see the results they expect. Successful people handle this by delegating work and hiring professionals to help them accomplish their goals.

This is also important because social media content is not just about posting the same trending news everyone is posting or creating content to publish something every day. The only way for your posts to become relevant and viral is to make sure that everything you post is going to provide top quality.

The only way to do this is by coming up with fresh and useful content, but you need to conduct market research before you can decide what to write about. Then, you also need to make sure that the content is easy to understand, original, and extremely appealing in terms of textual and graphical content.

8. Have a content plan

When you decide to start creating content for social media, you are going to find it extremely difficult to be able to do this with consistency all year long. Even being consistent with quality content for a few weeks can prove to be an extremely difficult thing.

This is the reason why you need to make sure that you can come up with a viable content plan. This is easier said than done when you have so many things to worry about and you can't be on top of every aspect of the business.

A good content plan will be essential for you to achieve the best results, which means you need to find a viable solution that is practical and cost-effective.

A team of social media marketing professionals has carefully structured this, and they ensure that each day is going to include a suggestion that is ideal based on the month and the day of the month.

9. Good Design matters

The way your posts look is going to be just as important as the content they include, and this can be more relevant in platforms like Instagram that rely on canvas-styled messages for audience engagement.

This process can also be a little difficult to handle as it requires time for you to come up with enough design ideas. Keep in mind that copyright issues are becoming more frequent than ever before, so you can't just take any image from the internet to use it for your messages.

Making sure that you can create appealing posts with those images is going to be extremely important.

You will need to invest a significant amount of time in this process, and this is not a viable solution for most business owners who are too busy to handle everything. The main issue with this is that you can't skip this part of the process because it will be essential for engagement.

A great way to make sure that your designs will be optimal for your campaigns is to use great templates. The solution is to implement 360 Social Media Post Templates.

They have created the ultimate collection of Instagram canvas templates that will ensure a truly diverse selection. When you have so many great templates at your disposal, you are never going to have to worry about searching for quality designs again.

10. Post frequently

There is no better way to stand out from the competition in social media than to be more active than they are, but there is a downside to this if you don't do it right. Some business owners try to do this by posting every day, but they sacrifice quality when they do this, and that hurts them more than it helps their business.

The biggest concern when you sacrifice quality is that your followers are not going to see you as a truly outstanding source of information. This could lead many of them to unfollow you and look for other sources of information that are more consistent with quality.

The key is to find the balance between quality and consistency, but you should never sacrifice quality just to post frequently. This means that if you are only able to produce one quality publication each week, it is better to do this than to post five times per week with rehashed and unoriginal content that your audience won't like.

11. Post at the right time

There is actual science to the process of posting your content on social media and achieving the highest engagement possible. You need to consider many factors if you want to be able to do this properly. The time of the day, the target audience and their most common time to be online, the day of the week, the holidays that may be happening around a day or during any specific day, and many other details.

This type of calculation can mean the difference between a post that is seen by a handful of people and a post that is seen by hundreds or even thousands of people. Every single time you post something new, you need to consider this if you want to make the most out of each post.

12. Use quality hashtags

The use of hashtags has always been something that confuses many people when they are trying to use them for their post engagement. One of the main things to consider when this happens is that people are very likely to create hashtags without really considering the reasons why they will use them and how they will use them in their content.

13. Optimize Your Profile for Search

This is also a huge thing to consider because your profile is going to be the first thing that most potential clients or customers are going to see when they search for what they want. By having a truly attractive and engaging profile, you will be increasing your chances of being found by the people who are looking to buy what you are selling.

Optimizing your profile is not just about words but also about your choice of images, colors, and themes. Many factors will play a role in the appeal of your profile, so make sure that you take the time to do this the right way.

14. Interact with your followers

This is something that you really need to work on because it will make a huge difference in the level of trust and loyalty that you are able to create with your target audience.

It's always a good idea to use live streaming to show your face to your audience and have interactions with as many of them as possible.

When you do this, you create a sense of familiarity, and your audience can start to see you as a friend and not just someone who is trying to sell them something. This personalized engagement will play a huge role in your ability to retain your audience and boost conversions.

15. Diversify your content type

One of the biggest mistakes that people make on social media is that they only create a certain type of content. Some will post text with an image, others will do streams online, and some will post audio clips.

The best approach to any social media promotional effort is to be diverse and to combine all types of media with your content.

The more you diversify your content type, the more it will maintain that fresh appeal with your audience, and this is also important. With that said, do not forget that the main thing to keep in mind at all times is to maintain quality above everything else.

It has been proven that video has grown in popularity on social media, but never forget the power of a good social media post that contains text with an attractive image. Mix things up and keep your audience engaged with quality content, and the follower count will grow much faster.

16. Promote your social media in your network

Sometimes one of the best ways to get a good initial boost with your social media efforts is to simply consider the use of your existing network of people to promote your page. This is going to be a great way to gain a bit of momentum as you start to create content.

It is easier to be able to see results when you are able to find a number of initial followers who can interact with your posts and share them with their network. This creates an immensely powerful snowball effect that can lead to a quick rise in your follower count.

17. Collaborate with other influencers

Collaborating with other influencers is always a great way for you to boost your own presence and to start gaining more and more credibility in your niche. You should take the time to search for influencers that have audiences that will find your products or services appealing.

Once you are able to collaborate with them, you could end up finding a huge audience that is going to follow your content as well. This is a great strategy for faster social media growth, and ultimately, we all want to be able to see a rise in our follower count as the most important goal.

18.Take advantage of special events and holidays

Make sure that you take the time to anticipate the holidays and to prepare great content based on those specific holidays. This is going to prove to be extremely useful when you are trying to engage your audience during a specific season or event.

Social Media Optimization

Approximately 2.77 BILLION people use social media worldwide. These people use their preferred social network in a number of ways. Some simply look to be entertained by it, while others use it for research.

As a real estate agent trying to market to these people, you must ensure they find you when searching. Much like optimizing your website for search engines, you must optimize your profiles for social media.

How to Optimize Your Social Media Profile

You can optimize Facebook and Instagram in the same way. Each has a social profile you must complete. This is a requirement because it is how you will appear to users.

Before you write the information on the profile requests, you should do keyword research for social media. Yes, just like a website and doing keyword research for it, you need to do research for social networks.

Spend time searching the social network for what users are looking for on it. You can do this by typing some words into the search that pertain to your services. Remember, you are a real estate agent who wants people in your local area because if you market to people two states away from you, you won't gain any new leads. That's why when doing your research, filter the search for people in a certain city.

Look at the users that come up for the services you have searched for to make sure they are in the area of your office.

You can then look over their information and questions or comments they have made about certain services. Note certain attributes about them. For instance, you might take notes on:

- ☐ Age
- ☐ Questions
- ☐ Comments
- ☐ Male or Female
- ☐ Job/Career
- ☐ Parent/Single/Married/Dating

These attributes will help you as you create content for your social media feed because you want it to pertain to the audience on the social network.

As you're searching for different services on the social network, pay attention to the ones that are brought up the most. Those are the ones you want to optimize your social media profile for when writing it.

Once you know the services that people are discussing the most, you're ready to optimize your profile. There are certain keyword phrases you should always use as a real estate agent.

- realtor in <city>
- <City> real estate agent

This should be in your description. For example, "Mr. Dereck James is a realtor in New York City with a realty office in Manhattan."

The services you researched should be part of the description as well. To continue the description above, you can write something like: "Mr. Dereck James is a real estate agent in New York City with more than 10 years of experience in helping people find their dream homes and sell their houses."

You have identified many of your services in your descriptions, and they are the ones that are most important to people on the social network for that description. When people search for any combination of those keyword phrases, your profile will show up because it's relevant to their search. Because of this, they will take notice of your services, post on your social media feed, and then click through to your website.

The Importance of Optimizing Your Social Media Profile Regularly

Optimizing your social media profile should be done regularly. Our recommendation is every two months. The reason for this is because people change what they search for, and you want to make sure your profile is current with what people care about at the time.

An example of how searches change is that maybe teeth whitening isn't as important to people in the winter months because it's cold, and they aren't as concerned about the way they look.

However, as the weather warms up, they pay more attention to their body and their face and see that their teeth are not as white as they would like, so they are interested in whitening services.

Maybe teeth whitening is more popular in the spring and summer because it's a popular time for weddings, and brides and grooms want to improve their smiles because of all the pictures.

So, you may not include teeth whitening in your list of services in your description in the winter months but include it in the warmer ones.

You may ask, "Why wouldn't I just include all of my services all of the time? Then they are always available no matter when people search." This is a great question, and it's valid.

However, social profile descriptions are often limited, so it's not always possible to add all services. Also, people may call certain services by a different name, and you must include that exact name in your description, or you may not come up in a search.

For instance, people may search for clear braces more than they search for Invisalign, so you would want to have "clear braces" instead of "Invisalign" in your list of services.

If you're unsure how to optimize your social media profile correctly, turn to the experts. We can help you optimize your social media profile to give you maximum visibility on social networks. When you have this, you can bring prospects to your website to convert them into new clients.

50 Most Engaging Content You Can Publish on social media

Great content can not only bring you more website visitors from search engines, but it can also bring you more potential buyers or sellers from social media.

As the world is evolving, social media tends to be part of the marketing strategies for almost every brand. There is nothing more troublesome for a professional marketer than struggling to bestow people with a creative block.

Even a professional and expert marketer can fall into despair if he is pressed to fabricate an original design to be run like a social media campaign within a deadline.

So in this section, I want to share with you the 50 most engaging and viral content types you can create to post on your social media and website.

1. Infographics

Infographics tend to be a productive way to educate your audience with a ton of information about your company, your brand, or your product with the help of visuals. Visuals are a secret art towards success, as they come in handy with the ability to turn the boring statistics into eye-catching details and keep your audience hooked.

Whether it would be your infographic or a masterpiece of a curator, with a classy infographic, your audience will surely be drawn to your social media post, and due to the premium visual aspects of the infographic, the viewers will surely go through your post till the bottom.

2. Motivational Posts

Many people go through thick and thin regularly, and what lights the people's mood is a little motivation. When targeted to the right audience at the right time, a motivational post can generate a heap of engagement towards your social media account.

These motivational posts can be easily designed by referring to the currently trending topic, but what will make your motivational post stand out from the average motivational posts is the choice of your words, as the words are the best tool to stop someone from giving up easily and can keep them going on strong on their path to success.

3. Long Articles

Just to be the term, long articles are referred to the inspirational stories or the experiences of celebrities or influencers who share their life experiences with the people to educate their audience about their day-to-day struggles.

As long articles tend to liberate & educate entrepreneurs and inspire them with their life struggles and experiences, this social media post can grab a wide range of traffic towards your post and hence can prove to be fruitful for generating leads and followers.

4. Plan Cohesive Campaigns

Building a complete campaign proves to be an effective way to drive a message home. Many people struggle to maintain their social media posts effectively as they remain dependent on their one-off posts. Building up a complete campaign will help you to stay organized.

Writing a post on the fly can prove to be tough and a hurdle to be done within a specific deadline; hence running a social media campaign will generate enough traffic to your post but will also help you to be effective social media content.

The campaigns can be either a series of posts to promote your product or a chain of branded posts that carries a consistent hashtag or a message.

5. The blog post of your company

Does your business contain a blog? Then you need to consider the fact that how you can generate a good number of leads and traffic towards your blog!

Having said that, sharing your company's blog on your social media platform will prove to be fruitful content for your social media account, and side by side, your blog will get its publicity too.

6. Posts Showing Your Company's Culture

What can prove to be a much better way to showcase your business by sharing a post that reflects your company's culture?

In simple words, a culture post is an effective approach to portray the image of your business or educate people about what your business is about. This can be anything; either you can show behind the scenes what your employees do in their free time, or it can be an article to make people aware of the wellbeing of your business or product.

7. Industry News

When it comes to the popularity of the articles, the articles that keep people updated with the latest news tend to attract more traffic and hence get more shares than an average article.

If you'll make users aware about what's the latest gossip going on in your niche, or if you'll make people updated about the ongoing operations in your niche, then you surely might have found a way to attract more leads to your social media platform.

Creating industry news is no big deal nowadays. You need to follow up with the latest proceedings going on in your surroundings, convert them into your post, and simply tweet it.

8. Curated Content

Curated content is one of the simplest ideas to create a post for your social media platform. The term curated content simply means to share the contents of other people within your niche.

It happens that sometimes the post you want to share with your audience is already designed or written by other people.

Rather than converting or creating a post of your own, you can simply share their post and give them credit. The advantage of Curated content is that you don't need to create your own, and your social media will keep updated simultaneously.

9. Questions Posts

Everything you share on your social media doesn't need to be in the form of information or an article. Sometimes you need to prioritize the feedback of your people, as the thoughts and feedback of your customers are what will make your company grow.

A question is as simple as "What sort of content should I blog about next" is enough to generate a heap of engagement towards your post.

10. Posting videos or photos of your company

Visuals are the best option to make your social media update to be classy and eye-catching. As per the saying of the experts, visuals have been the most essential way to generate high engagements.

Just like the visuals, research shows that video tends to bring 135 percent greater organic reach. It's suggested that you should take advantage of this organic reach and post videos of your company or your product on your social media account to grab the attention of the viewers.

11. Customer Reviews and Testimonials

Every company or product has some dedicated fans. Let the voice of your fans be heard, as they're the people who make your product better with reviews and feedback.

You can design a comment or feedback of any of your valuable customers and can thank them for sticking around with your company or product and praise them for believing in your company or product.

Sharing customers and reviews will not only create amazing content for your social media account, but mentioning your customer in one of your posts will be a matter of great appreciation for him.

12. Quick Tips and Advice

Every individual is in search of tips and tricks that can help him while doing his daily chores. Besides sharing a long-dedicated article to educate your customers about your product and your company, you can grab their interest by posting helpful tips and tricks that will enable users to serve with your site or use your product proficiently.

Creating this tidbit proves to be an easy task for a social media manager; hence if you're finding anything to post within a suitable deadline, then these tidbits can be your viable pick.

13. Memes or GIFs

As the world is evolving, today's viewers need something more than average articles or information being shared without any entertainment for them. Memes or GIFs prove to be the most effective way to grab the attention of your audience and simultaneously share the information about your company or your product with elite humor.

Memes and Gifs are the languages of the modern audience and hence receive far more likes, shares, and retweets than an average social media post. Memes and Gifs add a fun spin to your plain and dry posts and make it too irresistible for your audience to skip through them.

You just need to make sure that the meme and GIF you're opting to post on your social media accounts are related to your company or your product.

14. Contest Posts

People nowadays love to take part in the social media contest that is held worldwide. A much bigger firm runs social media contests on their social media accounts and promises viewers a free giveaway.

This giveaway can be a little price cash as a token of appreciation, or it can either be free services of that company or product. The point is that this contest post grabs a lot of attention from the viewers and urges them to participate enthusiastically. These contest posts can surely be one of the best social media posts, leading you towards more followers.

You need to remain clear about the objective of the contest, think out the best possible way to make your audience participate in it.

15. Holiday Posts

No matter how successful a business you run or a highly demanded product you have, you need to post content on your social media account that would give people an idea about how you relieve your stress.

And what can prove to be a more attention-grabbing post than posting some aesthetic pictures of a holiday destination that the employees or the boss of the company are planning to go on?

By these posts, you'll surely generate a heap of engagement, and your audience will love the fact that the employees of your company are real people that love to take their days off to enjoy their lives.

16. Photos From Company Events

If you're done with our Cultural post idea and want to take a step ahead of that idea, then this could be a viable pick. You need to look for a couple of events your company has organized or participated in over the years.

Take out the pictures of that function and post them on your social media account with a caption of "Flashback". Not only will this educate people about the past of your company, but it surely will allow the company to relive that splendid day.

If this is not possible, if you're a company as a host to a charity event or fundraiser, your social media would be a great source to spread awareness of the events.

17. Post an Answer to a Commonly Asked Question

You must have received a ton of emails or direct messages on your social media platform where dozens of customers would have asked a ton of different questions. Instead of solving the queries of the users one by one, you can create a social media post that contains the answer to that relevant question to solve it all at once.

You should make sure that your answer should be a detailed one to clarify users with similar queries. Having said that, posting an answer to the commonly asked question will make your customers have a positive impact on your firm and will surely grab you a heap of engagement.

18. Start a Conversation with a Leader In Your Industry

Nowadays, the people that are in a higher position in their respective firms have started coming forward on social media to crosstalk with a fellow employee where they both discuss the operations and proceedings held at the company.

Cross-promoting by having a conversation with someone within your niche proves to be an essential way to spread awareness and information about your company or your product and hence can surely attract potential leads to your social media account.

19. Links to Free Resources

Everyone loves to get free stuff, whether you offer your viewers access to free eBooks, white papers, or other free useful content. Everything that comes for free will surely be appreciated by your audience.

Create a link that provides users with access to an ultimate bundle or a downloadable infographic that makes people aware of the proceedings and operations of your firm and proves to be a helpful resource for them to be used for further references.

Share and promote this link on your social media account so that it could be accessed by dozens of people, and hence would bring an optimum reach to your social media account.

20. Podcast Episodes

As the world is evolving, if you want to run your social media successfully and give tough competition to other developing brands, then you need to think of something more than articles to publish on your social media account.

Reading tons of information is no fun! Apart from being time-consuming, it can make your viewers super bored. Hence to grab their attention successfully, start a podcast of your own, and publish it on your social media account.

Podcast not only provides the audience's eyes a break but can prove to be a viable option to attract some potential leads.

21. New Job listings

Are you looking forward to expanding your team? then what can prove to be more fruitful than choosing your next new employee from one of your audiences.

Nobody will work with more hard work and dedication than one of your company's fans, who has witnessed your company grow and has been standing with your firm since day one. While posting a job list on your social media account, you precisely describe what positions you guys are hiring for.

22. Hiring Announcements and New Team Members

Once you post your new job listing post on your social media account, you'll probably get the right candidate for you within no time. Now take a step further in this regard; you can create a post to welcome the new member to your team.

In your post, you can share the qualifications, hobbies, and plans this new member has for your firm. In short, you can introduce the new member to your audience. This post will serve as a welcoming post for the new member; besides that, it will surely grab the interest of lots of potential leads.

23. "On This Day In History" Posts

What can prove to be a more classy and eye-catching post than keeping your viewers updated about how amazing your day went in previous times. Besides being one of the best content for making your social media amazing, this post will offer users to relive this best particular memory once again.

Find something that happened a year back at this exact date, and let your users know about it!

24. Event Promotion

Many popular firms and companies organized different types of events to promote their services or their products to the audience. However, how are your users supposed to know of an event if you don't share and promote it on your social media account?

The best way to promote your events on your social media accounts is by creating banners, interesting aesthetic logos and by using trending hashtags. This will not only be helpful to promote your event but would serve as a premium, and optimum post for your social media account for sure.

25. Live Videos

If you have been using your social media for years, you must know that most of the social media apps like Instagram, Facebook, Snapchat, etc., provide you with an opportunity to interact with your admirers and fans over the web by going live from your social media account.

But to go live, you need to consider the social media platform that'll prove to be fruitful for you and will be watched by a maximum number of people. While many people won't be active and will not be able to interact with you on your live video.

You should post that live video on your social media account. That will not only be the best content for your social media platform but also will enable users to interact with you in the comment section.

26. Promote Email Sign-Ups

If your company is organizing a webinar or demo to educate or brief youngsters on a particular topic, you'll need to let your audience know about it by posting eye-catching designs of sign-up forms for webinars or demos on your social media account with the finest detail of engaging content.

This post will surely help you to generate heaps of potential leads for your social media account, as well as help you to make your webinar successful.

27. Image Scrambles

Just to be particular, the term image scrambles means an image that is hard to read by your audience.

Many popular and well-known brands post the scrambled images on their social media accounts whenever they launch a new product in a market and allow people to guess what the scrambled image means.

Mainly, the audience and viewers love to scratch their heads to figure out what's behind your scrambled image. Hence having said that, image scrambles proves to be one heck of a post for your social media account.

28. Inspirational Quotes

Many social media marketers find inspirational quotes to be cheesy; therefore, they avoid using inspirational quotes, especially on their social media account. But if used correctly, then no other social media tends to be effective than posting inspirational quotes.

Your audience would love to read relatable quotes from the leader of your company. Hence, posting inspirational quotes will not only grab your audience's attention but will surely be the finest way to spread motivation and inspiration among your followers.

29. Company Accomplishments

Whether you agree with this fact or not, but your fans and your audience look after you just like your very own. They care about you and want you to succeed in every aspect of your life.

Having said that, what can prove to be more beautiful than sharing your achievements and success with your viewers and counting them in, in every victory of yours.

Whether it's an award that you or your company earns somewhere, or you completed one decade of your services, keep your audience included in your happiness!

30. Host a Twitter Chat

If you're looking forward to a social media post that connects you with your audience and brings loads of potential leads towards your social media platform, then hosting a Twitter chat can prove to be fruitful for sure.

Hosting a Twitter chat means providing your fans and audience to have a conversation and share their thoughts and reviews over one unique hashtag. Having said that, you can promote this new initiative on your social media account to make people aware of it and enable them to participate in the conversation effectively.

31. Social Media Polls

As you must have got to know by the heading, this review is about prioritizing what your audience wants to see on your social media account. Your audience always keeps some expectations from you, and what can prove to be more beautiful than making your next post according to the suggestions and advice of your fans and audience.

Hence you can post a question on your social media account that states " What do you think our next post should be"? This will engage your audience towards your post as the audience will share their thoughts with you in the comment section, and you'll surely be able to increase your potential leads.

32. How-to Videos

Besides going live or posting lengthy paragraphs to make people understand the functionality of your products or the services you offer, videos tend to be much easier to explain your agenda.

How to do videos are the videos that are created to explain to people how a particular feature or tool works. Not only this, these videos provide your audience with an in-depth look at your tool, and will most likely engage them to try this tool themselves.

Having said that, these videos will surely be the most engaging and most effective post to be posted on your social media platform ever.

33. Client Reviews

Reviews play an essential role in the life of the audiences, as whenever they need to purchase something, they will look after the reviews of the products first. Having said that, reviews are proven to be the sales driver of your services and hence would serve as one of the best ideas to create content for your social media account.

big difference and major improvement on my sells,
thanks your advices Mr NICK, they were so easy and
yet so powerful.
I really wish i knew you years ago. i'm sure you would
have saved me a lot of effort but now your tips and
tricks are graved in my brain.

Thanks a lot, glad to help 😊
♥ 1

let me know if you have any other questions

34. Images or Videos of Your Clinic

You often must have heard about this famous saying of a nobleman "The most attractive product sells the best." Having said that, if you want to grab the attention of your viewers towards your post and generate a heap of engagement towards your social media account, you should try to capture aesthetic pictures of your clinic and put them on your social media attractively.

35. Question/Answer session

While looking for a thing to be posted on your social media, you need to look at something more than visuals and long articles.

You need to consider the fact that the post you're about to post on your social media will be able to gather enough engagement or not?

Hosting a question-answer session on your social media platform can prove to be fruitful for you as it will enable your audience to ask and clarify their queries with you while being engaged in your social media post.

36. Spotify Playlists

Do your friends trust you for the great music choice you have? Well, then they would love to listen to something that you suggest! Sharing Music with friends is one of the best ways to discover new artists and new bands.

Sharing music is also one of the ways that can give you a reason to talk to someone! A person can learn better about their music choices as well!

Spotify has sharing tools that allow you to share your personalized playlists. If you have some fans, they would love to know what you are listening to!

37. User-Generated Content

If you have amazing fans, then it's only fair that you share fan-worthy content with them as well!

A lot of actors and influencers give "shout-outs" to the fans that do something related to their idol celebrity or leave amazing product reviews. Some examples that may include this type of Leads are when a fan posts a photo of them with some gear related to a celebrity or a brand. And to be very honest, it feels like a huge win! This is indeed one of the best ways.

38. Posts Telling about the Company's History

If you have been the one whose brand or company has been around for quite some time now, then you have a lot of history to share with your fans to get them to trust you better!

When people see the progress of a business from the place where it started to the place where it currently is, it leaves them motivated as well as they are inspired by your brand.

Sharing your history is a great way to do something amazing to keep your fans intrigued.

39. Company New Announcements

Sharing news with your fans can make them feel like they are a part of your company and is one of the best ways to generate better leads! Is your business currently moving, or do you have any news overall that needs to be shared company-wide?

What better way could there be than sharing the news publicly and let the people in on the news who care about them too? This way, you can get your fans to get excited too!

40. Create a Regular Series

Are you still in search of ways to create unrealistic leads, and the above options haven't clicked with you? This is one of the best options: to create a weekly series or a show. The two ways that you can do this are:

- By using the standard talk show format
- Bringing in a Star guest each week.

There are businesses such as Paste that are benefiting from this strategy.

41. Repurpose Blog Graphics

Designing new visual content for every individual social media post can be a lot of time and resource-consuming. Innovate a bit and use Blog Graphics with social media in mind!

If you want to be doing this, you need to create versions of your blog graphics rather accurately for the platform that you are going to be using. Using these Blog Graphics, you can even create whole campaigns!

42. Share How-to Videos

The Internet is known for helping people to make sense of something. By doing this, you can help people and make a positive image for your brand as you will be saving them the time and effort they would need to do without switching to a website to search for something that they want to get done!

If you are selling products, it will help a lot of your buyers find out how to operate your products!

43. Sharing the story of a patient:

People just love seeing and hearing a positive review. Do you have a patient that has nothing but positive things to say about you?

You can get that patient in on a case study that you are doing and then share it with your followers on social media!

44. Share a Survey

Surveys are one of the best ways to learn about your customers and get their feedback on many things. This will allow you to build stronger leads as well as allow you to see what you can do better to promote your business in a better way.

This will also make your followers feel special.

45. Promote a New Event

What better way could be than giving your audience details about something that is going to be launched shortly or some event that the company is going to arrange?

This will make your audience feel like they are a part of a closed-loop and will allow you to gain more leads and followers.

46. Share a Fill-in-the-Blank Post

As already mentioned above, making your audience feel like their opinion is valued can prove a lot healthier for you and make it easier for you to generate more leads and attract more clients.

If you are looking for ways to hear something from your fans, then a Fill-in-the-Blank post is the best option! This will allow you to hear the unique reviews and opinions of your customers.

47. Reshare Your Top Performing Posts

Doing something unique is not always the answer. One of the ways to generate better leads via social media is to share your greatest hits!

This will turn a lot of followers of your online into buyers hence bringing you profits! After all, everyone loves a positive and working solution.

48. Share Some Interesting Industry Research

In today's world, having up-to-date information and research is an important factor for being a step ahead of your competition. One way you could keep your followers intrigued and generate more leads is by sharing statistics that are related to your field!

In these statistics, you could give statistics on something that can be improved by using your products. Make sure that the statistics that you provide are accurate.

49. Preview a New Product or Event

One way for your fans and followers to love you more is to bring in the upcoming products. After all, everyone loves being looped in on something that is not known to the general population.

You can get a lot of new followers and clients by regularly sharing snippets of the new products and features that are going to be introduced in the near future. This will allow you to get more leads as your followers with visit your social media handles to see what's new.

50. Giveaways!

Freebies are one of the best ways to keep your followers attracted towards what you are selling. After all, who doesn't like freebies? One way to generate active leads and gain more clients is to incentivize your followers on social media by offering a freebie.

This will enhance your brand's products and will allow you to create a better reputation for yourself.

As an example, We have Sony: Sony offers a free customized theme for a PlayStation in the scenario that customers pre-order a game.

SPECIAL BONUS

Would You Like Our Team To Design A Custom Marketing Plan For Your Real Estate Business For Free?

Thanks for making it to the end; I hope you enjoy this book so far.

Now you have more ideas to generate more leads online.

But you may also want expert's opinions on marketing.

That's why I want to provide you with a free one-on-one strategy call.

What you are going to get:

One of our marketing experts will meet with you live using Skype and design a customized marketing plan specifically for your real estate business.

Once it's designed, we'll then build you a blueprint and a process map of it so you'll be able to deploy it at will.

Here's How It Works

We begin working before we ever meet.

First, you must complete an application form and tell us about your business.

We analyze your target market, spy on your competitors, and play "mystery prospects" by going through your website, fan page, and content as if we were a potential prospects.

Then We Meet, One-On-One.

We'll do it using Skype or phone, and we will discuss the things that need to be changed to attract more high-quality leads.

Again, everything is done custom and explicitly designed for your business after we've had a chance to ask you about your marketing process, revenue goals, and branding strategy.

There Is No Charge For This, and There Is No Catch.

...Which, of course, leads you to wonder, *"Why would you do all of this work for free?"*

Well, in the interest of full transparency, this is how I get clients.

A good percentage of the people I do this for end up asking us to manage their social media, build their websites and their sale funnel, write all their content, and set up their marketing campaigns.

When that happens, my team and I actually set up their account, built all the web pages, built the follow-up campaigns, wrote the content, set up ads, and implemented everything <u>for</u> the client.

So that's my "hidden motivation" for doing this. However...

THIS IS NOT A "SALES PITCH IN DISGUISE"

Far from it.

You'll get no pressure to become a client because we let the value of the free work speak for itself.

The marketing plan we design for you, for free, will be absolutely transformational for your business.

I guarantee it.

The bottom line is, that we'll design you an amazing marketing plan for free, and we'll even give you a blueprint of it so you can deploy it at once.

After that, you might want to become a client. Or not.

I won't pressure you either way.

If you'd like a free customized marketing plan and blueprint, click the link below to get started.

Go to <u>http://soldouthouses.com/call</u>

to book your free strategy call.

RESOURCES

Thanks for taking this book; the following are some resources that can help you take your real estate business to the next level

1. The Ultimate Real Estate Marketing Checklist (Free)

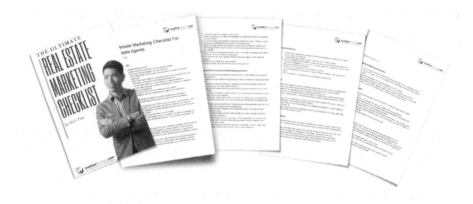

Get 86 proven real estate marketing ideas
to generate more leads online

Please go to https://soldouthouses.com/checklist
to download your free checklist

2. Our Digital Marketing Services

Want my team to take care of your internet marketing for you?

Visit Our site at https://services.soldouthouses.com/ to see what you can do to bring your real estate marketing to the next level

3. 150 done-for-you real estate infographics

Get your social media content ready in the next few minutes.

You can get your infographic package at https://soldouthouses.com/infographics.

4. 360 real estate social media post templates

Create professional social media content
quickly with those templates

You can get those templates at
https://soldouthouses.com/socialmediaposttemplates

5.360 real estate ad templates

Create professional social media ad images
quickly with those templates

You can get all templates at
https://soldouthouses.com/adtemplates

6. Ebook - 3-minute real estate ads

Get 30 done-for-you social media ad copy
swipe files for a huge discount.

You can grab your copy at https://soldouthouses.com/3minads

7. My Sold Out Houses online store

Get everything you need to succeed with real estate marketing

You can visit our store at https://store.soldouthouses.com

Made in the USA
Las Vegas, NV
12 December 2024

13953648R00085